D0782462

Dependent Care and the Employee Benefits Package

Dependent Care and the Employee Benefits Package

Human Resource Strategies for the 1990s

LouEllen Crawford

QUORUM BOOKS

New York • Westport, Connecticut • London

Library of Congress Cataloging-in-Publication Data

Crawford, LouEllen.
  Dependent care and the employee benefits package : human resource
strategies for the 1990s / LouEllen Crawford.
    p.   cm.
  Includes bibliographical references.
  ISBN 0–89930–465–6 (alk. paper)
  1. Employer-supported day care—United States. 2. Parental leave—
United States. 3. Work and family—United States. I. Title.
HF5549.5.D39C73   1990
658.3′8—dc20   90–32724

British Library Cataloguing in Publication Data is available.

Copyright ©1990 by LouEllen Crawford

All rights reserved. No portion of this book may be
reproduced, by any process or technique, without the
express written consent of the publisher.

Library of Congress Catalog Card Number: 90–32724
ISBN: 0–89930–465–6

First published in 1990

Quorum Books, 88 Post Road West, Westport, CT 06881
An imprint of Greenwood Publishing Group, Inc.

Printed in the United States of America

The paper used in this book complies with the
Permanent Paper Standard issued by the National
Information Standards Organization (Z39.48–1984).

10 9 8 7 6 5 4 3 2 1

Contents

90-6108

Preface

This is a book about so many of us who hold down jobs and, at the same time, are positioned in some kind of dependency relationship between the older and younger generations. It is about demographic and social changes taking place that have serious implications for policy formation and for the way employers formulate their benefits packages. I put, up front, how best to address these changes in the workplace.

Chapter 1 is an exposition of these changes and their effects, changes I believe to have generated a crisis of dependency. I describe from personal experience, but mostly from research, the consequences of being a member of the labor force and the "sandwich generation"—what it means to the individual and what it means to that institution called work. Specific changes referred to are that we are getting older and living longer, women are entering the labor force in record numbers, single parenthood is becoming more common, young people are returning to the once-empty nest, and sex role stereotypes are being altered. The results of these changes to macro-society are to leave a growing number of younger and older "dependents" without the traditional mode of care, and to put pressure upon individuals and institutions to fill in for tradition.

Chapter 2 offers several rationales upon which industries can base their attention and adaptations to these changes. It is my intention to make a strong argument against apathy to these changes and for industries getting on the dependent care assistance bandwagon in order to retain valuable employees, to cut down on absenteeism and tardiness, and to be able to attract highly productive workers to their labor pools. The outcome of this effort will be increased productivity, and productivity is what doing business is all about.

Chapter 3 describes in some detail employee dependent care assistance policies already operating and identifies firms in which these policies are operational. Chapter 4 is a discussion of the survey I conducted of over three hundred U.S. industries from which I attempted to discover the kinds of industries having these policies, the location in the country of these firms, the type of dependent care benefits policies that firms have, and the extent to which policies are being accessed by workers.

Chapter 5 suggests future prospects for dependent care assistance to employees who are in a caregiver role. Pending legislation at the federal level suggests that businesses of a certain size may be required to provide parental leave *at least* on an unpaid basis. Dependent care assistance for fathers is an idea and practice that is catching on. Any way we look at it, we cannot avoid recognizing, unless we are socially blind, that dependent care assistance is an issue of the 1990s. Articles appear almost regularly in local newspapers, *The Wall Street Journal*, and in popular magazines concerning this issue. Private sector involvement in the issue is being encouraged by states and the federal government by offering tax credits to industries that provide child care assistance. Political support for adult day care is emerging, although slowly.

Chapter 6 is a discourse on an agenda of future concerns in the dependent care assistance area. Attention is focused on family matters as they are affected by education, wage compensation, and labor force participation. Changes in sex role stereotypes and how these will continue to affect fathers taking leave, and society's attitude toward single fatherhood are issues raised in this chapter. Underuse of employer tax credits to be allocated for the provision of dependent care services and of dependent care assistance provisions already in place is another concern of this chapter. The quality and quantity of day care centers is another problem area addressed. Manifestations of the dependency burden on the elderly, children, and caregivers are reiterated from Chapter 1 because of their great significance and because of the argument they make for greater public and private attention to this matter.

In researching this book, I was struck anew by the shortsightedness of this country's approach to its problem areas. That is, rather than being in a proactive, before-the-fact mode, we seem in most cases to be reactive and, as such, not to be in full control of the outcomes of our actions. This shortsightedness has frequently led us down the path of most—rather than least—expense and has caused undue suffering on the part of many. A case in point is Medicare. At least some people have been getting catastrophically ill since the beginning of time, yet the catastrophic illness clause in the Medicare policy (although it has been rescinded) did not exist for more than 20 years after the enactment of the Medicare mandate. Our reaction to the need for adequate day care is another case in point. In spite of all our high-tech prognostication, a plethora of "popular" literature on the topic, alarms sounded calling for a greater response, and the head-wagging behind closed and open doors of policymakers' offices, there continues to be an ever-growing shortage of affordable and satisfactory day care. Day care provision has become, in many cases, a shot-in-the-dark, patchwork, catch-as-catch-can reality; licensing procedures, follow-up, and regulations are, in far too many cases, inadequate and slipshod.

The reader will find practical and useful ideas for dealing with the dependent care issue in this book. Many of you will find yourselves being described for, if you are in a dependency crisis, you could have written parts of this book. Both employees and employers are in much the same boat with regard to the dependency issue, and I suppose there is some comfort in that fact. For, although we may be heading in different directions in our careers and lives, being a dependent caregiver is a leveler.

Acknowledgments

The process of writing a book of this sort describes a cooperative effort that usually begins with a key person. My key person is one to whom I owe unbounded thanks, Janice Marie, head librarian at Regis College in Colorado Springs, Colorado. She suggested titles and resource groups to enable me to begin my research. Key titles to which she referred me and groups to whom I am indebted for their own research are the Conference Board and the Catalyst Group. Janice's alert and able assistants, Ann Brown and Barbara Ivey, identified, located, and acquired a vast array of research material during the past year.

Richard Robinson, CPA and professor of economics and finance at Regis College, Colorado Springs, was my *Wall Street Journal* watcher, my conscience stimulator and sounding board, kindest critic, and chief-encourager-of-floundering incentive. Bob Stringer of Business Referrals worked with my survey data making attractive charts and graphs to be photographed for the book. Henry Schodorf, local businessman and professor at Regis College, succumbed to an interview, explaining how the human factor of production is just as important as capitalization and how flexibility of work scheduling is needed in today's work world. Lane Johnson, personnel manager at Tiernay Metals in California, also granted me an interview during one of her visits to a neighbor of mine.

My initiation into the plight of sandwich generation members took place as I researched the topic for use in a seminar for women making up a Colorado branch of the National Organization, Women of Las Hermanas. It is from presenting this seminar and from the realization that I, too, am a member of this generation that my interest in the topic was sparked.

Upon request, many called to give and/or sent me information on particular dependent care assistance programs in their companies, and to these thoughtful and helpful people I owe a debt of gratitude. Representative Patricia Schroeder (D-CO) sent me an abundance of material on parental leave legislation, and Sharon Triolo in Schroeder's Denver office clarified some points for me. Loretta M. Kollar, director and day care consultant of the Learning Center at Excel-Nyloncraft in Mishawaka, Indiana, Michael J. Duda, vice president of personnel at Remington Products in Bridgeport, Connecticut, and Janet M. Haflich, compensation analyst at Union Planters National Bank in Memphis, Tennessee, broadened my knowledge with their information packets about what their industries are doing for their employees. Karen Liebold, director of program development at the Stride Rite Children's Centers in Cambridge, Massachusetts, Kathleen Russell of the Benefits Department of PepsiCo, a spokesperson at U.S. West Communications of Englewood, Colorado, and Amy L. Wilson, benefits communications specialist at Pitney Bowes, all generously shared dependent care assistance information with me.

In the final moments of my research effort, Dr. Boris Gertz, a private clinical consultant in Denver, and Sharon Williams, a consultant at the Technical Support Services at Digital Equipment Corporation in Colorado Springs, came to my rescue. Sharon, a former student of mine at Regis College, elaborated and gave me written information on Digital's participation in a national teleconference on elder caregiving and the corporation's "brown bag" seminar session on the topic. With their help I was able to lay to rest my research effort on behalf of the book.

Sandra Matthews of the University of Colorado at Colorado Springs, Margaret Brubaker, and Pam Summers, All-In-One Secretarial, a neighbor, made up for my lack of incentive and/or expertise on behalf of the manuscript production process. Sandra drew my sample, a job I try to avoid doing at almost any cost, Margaret typed and edited the first draft of the first chapter, and Pam quickly and efficiently typed the final draft of the entire manuscript.

Finally, for my friends and family who somehow and in varying degrees put up with my mostly mental and sometimes physical absence from them, I am grateful.

1

Defining the Challenge

For the past several years, significant developments have taken and are taking place with regard to employee benefits and compensation. These developments have emerged as a result of some rather dramatic but slowly evolving trends in the composition of the formal labor force. In turn, these trends typically are seen as resulting from subtle but concrete changes in demographics and society as a whole.

The developments are viewed as a response to what can be termed the compensation issue of the 1990s—that issue that addresses the needs of a growing number of people in our workforce. These developments can be seen as an almost revolutionary force, a subtle but gentle "revolution" not traceable to any abrupt change. The "revolution," according to Smith (1979), can be attributed to the attractiveness of paid labor to women, especially those who are educated, an increase in white collar employment, changes in sex role attitudes, and inflation. Increasing unemployment of men and urbanization have also contributed to this trend.

Addressing the needs of this growing number of people has become an issue of the 1990s because of the divergence of opinion as to how to address these needs and with regard to the variety of reactions of employers and employees to the solution. Titles of articles in such periodicals as *The Wall Street Journal* infer the timeliness of the issue—"Boss's Backing

Vital to Family Benefits" (January 10, 1989); "Elder Care Needn't Keep Employees Out of the Office" (August 8, 1988); and "Firms Begin Support for Workers Who Look After Elderly Relatives" (July 6, 1988). In *Across the Board* (June 1986) we see "Eldercare: The Employee Benefit of the 1990s?"

The end but not the final result of this revolution, and the issue to which these articles speak, has been an ever-growing number of members of the labor force who qualify as members of what has come to be known as the "sandwich generation." These are people, both men and women (although the largest proportion are women), who are in a life-squeeze, to whom Miller refers as comprising the "command generation"—people making up a "coalition of nuclear families in a state of . . . dependence in which members exchange services" (1981: 420). Dependency, for purposes of this study, is inferred by one or more of the following needs: emotional-psychological, economic, physical, and social. Dependents are members of the younger generation—children and even young adults—and the older one—parents and grandparents. Many of this sandwich generation are those who are simultaneously occupied with careers and dependent care responsibilities, being sandwiched between two generations.

People of the sandwich generation are finding themselves trapped, sometimes through no volition of their own, in a dilemma of commitment to both work and domestic-family responsibilities. These responsibilities pertain to providing some kind or kinds of care simultaneously to members of the generations on either side of them. The care given to dependents covers a wide range and variety of responsibility. (It is usually women who honor these responsibilities.) One topic covered in chapter 2 is how these responsibilities impinge upon workers' performance. They do impinge, to which much research attests. This cause-and-effect relationship is just beginning to be addressed. A discussion of why it should be addressed comprises the main body of rhetoric in the next chapter. The chapter proposes that it is in the best interests of both private and public sector businesses that attention be given to and action be taken on behalf of the "phenomenon."

Being simultaneously occupied with both work and family has meant an increasing but varying response to, and interest in, the problems associated with caregiving responsibilities on the part of employees and employers, both from private and public spheres. In the local, state, and national political arenas, dependent care policies are being hotly debated and are sure to be debated through the 1990s (Finegan 1989). In the past these policies have taken the form of parental leave bills, and the 1989 version of both House and Senate, and long-term health care proposals. Briefly, the parental leave bills (described in detail in chapter 5) would provide job security for employees taking up to ten weeks in a two-year period of unpaid leave to care for a sick child or parent. During the leave employers would be required to continue medical and health insurance already provided. After the leave, the employee must be reinstated in the same job or a comparable one with no loss of salary, benefits, or seniority.

The federal government's first commitment to day care came with New Deal legislation in the form of the National Recovery Act, which mandated, among other things, emergency nursery school for children of needy, unemployed families or for those in neglected or underprivileged homes. Funded under this mandate were 1,900 child care centers serving 75,000 children. However, as employment increased in the late 1930s and federal funds were withdrawn, these centers began to close.

Child care needs again became of enormous concern to many government agencies during World War II as well as to employers who wanted to retain trained workers. Over 3,000 child care centers were federally funded under the Communities Facilities Act and the Lantham Act; some 130,000 children were accommodated in these centers, a number far greater than the number that could be comfortably accommodated. At the end of the war, 2,800 of these centers were terminated.

Employment practices affecting pregnant women were first scrutinized by the federal government during World War II when one-third of the nation's labor force was women. Six weeks of prenatal leave and two months of postnatal leave were recommended, as were job protection and the acknowledgment of seniority rights. But with these recommendations, women's employment circumstances changed only slightly, leave was often mandatory and unpaid, and women often lost seniority and lost accrued benefits by going on leave.

In the 1960s the President's Commission on the Status of Women began to urge job- and seniority-protected paid maternity leave, but these urgings did not result in legislation.

Rights of pregnant workers were addressed in Title VII of the Civil Rights Act and were further explicated by the Equal Employment Opportunity Commission in 1972 with the statement that temporary disabilities to which job leave, health or disability insurance, seniority, and reemployment could accrue were to include disabilities resulting from pregnancy, miscarriage, abortion, childbirth, and recovery therefrom. Twenty-two states and the District of Columbia followed suit, passing legislation requiring coverage for pregnancy and pregnancy-related disabilities similar to that provided for other temporary disabilities (Zigler and Frank 1988). In a case argued in front of the Supreme Court in 1977, employers were given the right to refuse sick pay to women who are unable to work because of pregnancy and childbirth but disallowed employers divesting those women who took maternity leave of accumulated seniority.

A coalition of women's civil rights, church, and organized labor groups, who urged Congress to overturn the Supreme Court decision arguing that protective laws for women would exclude them from equal protection under the law, was instrumental in getting the Pregnancy Discrimination Act (PDA) passed. This act pertained to rights grounded in the civil rights language of the 1960s. The PDA provides protection for women who work for employers offering disability insurance benefits (although only 40 percent of all women receive the type of maternity benefits that guarantees job protection and partial wage replacement).

Both public and private responses represent the liberal and conservative sides of the ideological spectrum as well as the middle-of-the-road stance. Conservatives, in their belief in minimum governmental intervention, maintain that it is not in the best interests of businesses to involve themselves in the social welfare of employees. Conservatives feel that a person's social and economic circumstances are of the person's own making, and thus the individual needs to "own up" to them. Liberals, in contrast, argue that it is government's responsibility to provide needed social welfare in these areas. It is everyone's right, furthermore, to expect the government to do so. For example, labor, having "worked hard" for the forty-hour week and an eight-hour day, argues that practices applied to ease the family work dilemma such as flextime scheduling would undermine the cohesion of labor. Corporate managers seem more receptive to the problems of elder caregivers than to child caregivers. Perhaps this is because managers are more likely to be older and, therefore, are caring for elders rather than children. The midposition sees a wedding of private and public responsibility, claiming that neither the government nor private sector enterprises have carried in the past the burden of providing social welfare alone, nor should it.

It is the purpose of this study, first of all, to describe this sandwich generation as well as the demographic, social, and labor market trends that have created it. An examination of these trends in terms of their effects on labor force performance factors and the response of many industries to these trends are described. What these trends hold for the future is addressed.

Material on demographic, social, labor, and economic characteristics and trends and the effects from them is taken from a plethora of literature representing a vast array of texts, periodicals, magazines, journals, pamphlets, government documents, reference works, yearbooks, and newspapers. Prospects for the future are suggested by examining literature on proposed legislation and pending action on the part of policymakers in the private and public sectors. The examination of industries' response to trends—specifically the response to the influx of workers belonging to the sandwich generation—takes as its point of departure a personally conducted mailed survey done in 1989 of 325 industries listed in the April 25, 1988, issue of *Forbes*.[1] The results of the survey were tabulated and interpreted by this author. This interpretation and the projections based on it make up the main thrust of this study and, as such, represent the uniqueness of this book.

CREATION OF A SANDWICH GENERATION

The demographics, sociology, and economics of dependency have high explanatory power for the number of dependents being left without care by a "traditional" in-home caregiver, and the number of persons entering the circumstances of caregiving. (These trends portend an increasing need for outside-the-home dependent care programs.) The first of these is the rapid rate at which women of all ages are entering the labor force, especially those under 35 years old. By 1987 two-thirds of married women 20 to 34 years of age were in the workforce. Since 1970 the greatest increase in entrants has been among those under 35 with children under 3 years old (Kammerman 1980). Today, 64.8 percent of those mothers with children under 18 years of age are working, whereas 54.4 percent with youngsters less than 6 years old are also working. It has been estimated that by the year 2000, 75 percent of all women between the ages of 45 and 60 will be in the labor force. Two-thirds of those hired by firms will be women. A corollary of women entering the labor force is the increase in two-income households, creating a need for stay-at-home help for dependents. For the first time in history, the number of two-income families outnumbers single-income families (Sullivan 1981).

Explanations for the increasing entry of women into the labor force are numerous. Labor market needs and women's perceptions of their "proper" roles help explain this phenomenon. During the era when the United States was beginning to industrialize, workers were needed in the secondary manufacturing sector of the labor market, and so the largest proportion of the labor force was in jobs in that sector. As the country grew in economic and other terms, the demand began to shift away from the secondary manufacturing sector toward the third or tertiary sector in which white collar, professional, technical, managerial, proprietorship, clerical, sales, and services jobs are located.[2] Workers in these jobs are known as white collar salaried workers as opposed to blue collar workers who are occupational incumbents in the manufacturing-industrial and agricultural sectors and are wage workers.[3] Kocka (1980) points out that advanced industrialization in all societies is marked by an increase in the proportion of white collar workers to blue collar workers.

It is the "attractiveness" and creation of white collar work that partially explains women's increasing labor force participation. Its attractiveness is seen in its goodness-of-fit between work roles and domestic role requirements. This is especially and particularly true of jobs in the lower white collar category such as routine clerks and sales workers, and professions such as nursing, librarianship, teaching, service jobs, and social work. In both these kinds of jobs and in domestic tasks, the role requirements of "workers" are similar. The time demands of the career of teaching, for example, often dovetail rather nicely with time demands on the home front, especially if the worker's children are of school age.

Kocka attributes the growth of the number of white collar jobs in the tertiary sector to several phenomena, including increasing bureaucratization, the separation of ownership and managerial functions, an increasing division of labor as a result of increasing specialization, the mechanization and application of science to the production process, and an extension of the contact between the state and the economy. These phenomena are the very ones that have created what John Naisbitt in his book, *Megatrends*, calls our Information Society.[4]

At the same time that women are entering the labor force in increasing numbers, our mortality rate is decreasing and more people are living longer. This "graying of America," the result of remarkable strides made in medical technology as well as the onset of the fitness craze, combined with a heightened awareness of good nutritional practices, health maintenance, and preventative medicine, has increased our elderly population and thus our dependency ratio.[5] The elder dependency figure has increased from 14 (for every 100 adults of working age) in 1950 to 19 in 1988; in the year 2010 there will be 20 "dependent" elders for every 100 adults of working age, and 32 in the year 2030 (Robertson 1987). Theoretically, dependency means that a number of supposedly nonworking elders are being supported in some fashion—through Social Security taxes, for example—by working adults and other public policy-generated programs to which workers contribute through payroll deductions and such.

In real numbers, we see that presently about 12 percent of the U.S. population is 65 years or older, whereas in 40 years or so, this proportion will increase to 20 percent. The fastest growing age cohort is that of 85-year-olds and older. An increase of elderly aged 95 and over from 2.6 million to 13.5 million by the year 2040 is predicted. Increasing longevity needs to be factored into this conceptual scheme as well: Americans who are 65 years old now, on average, have 16 more years to live. The number of 40-year-olds with at least one surviving parent increased from 70 percent in 1900 to more than 95 percent in 1985. These numbers mean that more of us have surviving parents who may possibly be dependent upon us. As a matter of fact, the average senior citizen requires 18 years of "special care"; most of the financial burden for this care falls on the younger generation, despite Medicare and Social Security availability.

A social trend noted by various commentators is swelling the ranks of the sandwich generation, to wit, it is not uncommon now to find that a member of this generation is one with older-than-teenage children at home as many of these young adults are returning to the nest, however temporarily. Lawrence Kutner (1988) admits that the reasons more young adults are returning home, especially those with middle class and upper middle class backgrounds, are yet obscure. Conjecture has it that many of these people, having been raised during the permissive 1960s, are finding it hard to cope with such adversities as unemployment, the failure to find a job paying a salary commensurate with one's aspirations, a depressed and highly competitive labor market, and a mismatch between what one is trained and educated to do and the type of occupation for which one must settle.

The number of "incompletely launched" young adults, as Schnaiberg and Goldenberg (1989) call them, has been fluctuating for both sexes, but the phenomenon is more true of men than of women, depending upon age. Glick and Lin (1986) found that of those 18 to 29, 34 percent were living with parent or parents in 1970; in 1984 this proportion grew to 37 percent. Schnaiberg and Goldenberg found that, in 1985, 7.8 percent of females 25 to 29 years old were living with their parent(s); in 1988, 8.6 percent of them were doing so. For males, these proportions were 16.6 percent and 19.1 percent, respectively. Heer et al. (1985) tell us that in 1970 approximately one-quarter of all 18-to-34-year-olds lived in their parents' households; by 1983 nearly one-third were doing so.

Further evidence that there are more dependent young adults is that there is a decline in the number of individuals who have their own families of procreation. This decline, between 1960 and 1983, has taken place with those between 18 and 34 years of age (Heer et al. 1985).

Schnaiberg and Goldenberg (1989) note changing behavior patterns in young adults in their returning to or staying at the home of their parents. They called these young adults incompletely launched in that they have not, for various reasons, become self-sufficient people. This phenomenon has social, economic, and developmental roots. With this type of behavior there is deviance from parental expectations that children will physically separate from their parents. In many cases, there are attempts made to fulfill these expectations that often are met with failure. Disappointment on the part of parents, if it occurs, may be based on social norms about when it is "proper" for a young adult to become independent. Therefore, when the failure to become self-sufficient occurs, parents will often take it personally rather than seeing it as resulting from social and economic factors.

Ideal-typical expectations that white, middle class parents usually have are that they are to provide intensive support of a child until the child reaches young adulthood and to raise the child to be independent. The creation of one's own family of procreation sometime, (usually) soon after graduation from high school or college, is yet another parental expectation. In other words, doing it by the numbers, just as parents might have done themselves, is what is expected by these parents of their children.

Social and economic bases for young adults staying in or returning to the home are that, for one thing, there is an education squeeze in which there are fewer "slots" in colleges for young adults aspiring to a college education. Greater family debt incurred because of the rising costs of a college education is another basis. In our present labor market, there tends to be less stability in career employment as well.

Educational spiraling could be a reason for young adults not leaving home as conventional wisdom would have it. Educational spiraling is a condition in the labor market by which more and more companies are demanding an increasing level of education on the part of their potential employees. The condition of credentialism speaks to this situation. Educational spiraling keeps young adults in school longer, getting the education their future employers will require, and makes them, therefore, dependent upon their family of origin for a longer time.

Another basis for young adults returning home or not leaving home at all is delayed marriage. Economic trends have tended to depress marriage rates over the past few years. This may be more true of women than it is of men; delaying marriage tends to keep young adults from moving out and establishing their own homes. Another factor to consider is that more mothers are not getting married. Bernstein (1989) notes that this may be due to young men not being able to afford marriage. Real average incomes of young men have fallen since the 1960s, and a growing number of them do not earn enough to support a family. For many, having low-paying jobs is the reason some young men postpone marriage or do not marry at all. The marriage market, under this condition, is less attractive to both men and women. In fact, marriage rates have fallen the most for men with little education and/or low-paying jobs.

Reticence to marry may be another factor discouraging young adults from leaving home. This reticence can come from a fear of marital disruption in this day when the divorce rate is very high and from the fear of dating because of AIDS. In the case of young adults of parents who themselves are divorced, there is often reluctance to "take a chance."

In Susan Littwin's excellent book, *The Postponed Generation*, reasons are given for the growing-up-later syndrome. Even though these kids (who grow up at a later age) have had expensive, even extensive, education and many material and social advantages, they have grown up confused, unfocused, and dependent in many cases. "Adulthood was turning out to be a crisis of confused expectations" (1986: 15). These expectations are partially a function of parents not having told kids that life is tough, that they are not necessarily entitled to instant status, expensive equipment, important and meaningful work, or limitless choices.

During the 1960s when these kids were growing up, Americans were a people of great optimism, almost to the point of euphoria: young pilots were being put into capsules and shot into space; the student power movement was underway; contraceptive devices making sexual encounters more "free" were reaching the age of sophistication; and confidence in major institutions such as banks, big corporations, and the medical and scientific communities ran high (Littwin 1986).

We were ebulliently experimental, believing that scarcity was a thing of the past, living in a consumer culture, and raising children in a Spock-ian, permissive way with an emphasis on "me" and individualism. Middle class parents reasoned with misbehaving children, parenting became a career, and the harder you worked at your career (and some interpreted "working hard" to mean giving much in the way of material goods), the greater the gain. The school became the arena in which parents could press for personal development, freedom, and creativity for their children (Littwin 1986).

But the maps to adulthood of the 1960s did not work in the 1980s and probably will not work in the 1990s. We have returned to a more traditional, conservative, basic social, political, and economic order. Entitlement, as a basic standard and mind-set lingers, however, with its inference of a right to alternative life styles, self-fulfillment, choice, and power, and this is what is giving the postponed generation fits of dependence, disillusionment, and lack of direction. There are not the jobs out there that college graduates have been told to expect, and the competition for those available is simply greater, sometimes overwhelming. For many, bleak job markets and job gaps are permanent fixtures.

In the early 1980s, with almost twice as many college graduates as there were job openings, those graduates were competing with high school graduates for jobs, creating educational spiraling. High school graduates became more unemployable, and the number of underemployed and overeducated grew. (In 1982 according to the Labor Department, 47 percent of college graduates 24 years old or younger were in jobs that did not require a college education.) Liberal arts and humanities majors were in the most disadvantaged position; those with technical, mathematical, engineering, and accounting degrees were in great demand. Relatively few college students sought career placement information before choosing their majors. Those who did seek advice and/or went on their instincts as to what the job market may portend for them in four years often found themselves "educated into a corner," having overspecialized and, therefore, in a mobility trap of sorts. Educational overspecialization narrows the job options, giving an overspecialist less latitude in jobs in the chosen field of study.

The college experience itself is at least somewhat different today than it was for the parental generation. Littwin suggests that college years today, in contrast to the 1960s, often are marked more by stress than intellectual and emotional growth. This stress is disillusioning but, important to the issue at hand, confuses the issues of self-reliance, direction, and purposiveness, often leaving the student with no lesson learned about the "real world." Add to that the observance that many students "live knee-deep in adolescent culture because they have no desire to be anything else. . . . They don't want to reach beyond the piping hot, fast fantasy of pop music, television and sports. To do so would mean identifying with adults and assuming responsibility" (Littwin 1986: 45).

Contributing to this stress is the fact that many students were not prepared well enough by their high schools for college courses. There is often confusion created by a multiuniversity atmosphere on some campuses with contingent competition to get into desired courses, a lack of privacy, large lecture sections, and a disregard for undergraduate education on the part of some professors. Then, too, high tuition costs force many to hold down a job as well and/or incur debt.

Why is returning home a phenomenon of young adults in their twenties and not of their parents? According to Littwin, one reason is that the parents lived in a world that valued them more. Grants, academic careers of all sorts, and fellowships proliferated. These are people whose parents, having lived through the Depression and World War II, had taught them that gratification would not be instant, that they would have to work hard and often long in order to be successful, that life would not be handed to them on a silver platter; they were taught that they were not "entitled." Furthermore, support from these parents' parents after college education usually was not offered except in rare cases of graduate school attendance.

Another trend with the potential to increase the size of the sandwich generation is found in the choice of many couples to postpone child bearing and rearing until their late twenties and early thirties. Levy (1987) contends that this choice increases the chances of couples being faced with child and eldercare responsibilities simultaneously. Most of the support for this contention is found in ethnograhpic form, that is, in personal history accounts of couples' choices about the life-style they chose to assume.

Yet another trend, and one that implies a need for the provision of outside-the-home dependent care programs, is an increasing shortage of household help. The entry of women into the labor force (and the fact that most caregivers are women) means a loss of in-family support for children and elders. Then, too, and coupled with the situation, is the tendency away from the extended family form, which has left the nuclear family "unsupported" in terms of in-home care.[6] The extended family form went by the wayside with the advent of industrialization and urbanization. Before industrialization, men conducted their businesses in the house with wife, children, and other family members present. Workplace and home were essentially the same and the generations lived under one roof, sharing in household as well as work tasks.

Historically, at the time when the country's economy was based on agricultural production, a significant function of the family was to provide security needs to its members. The extended family fulfilled this function nicely. In effect, the family, then, was life-health-disability insurance as well as a pension coverage. Every member, except for the very young and infirm elderly, contributed to the maintenance of the family, making each member an economic asset. At that time, approximately 95 percent of the population was engaged in agriculture. Actually, the last bastion of the full-time housewife is families where the husband's income is above average and the wife is not employed.

From the 1930s on, the working population moved out of the agricultural sector, into and through the industrial/manufacturing sector into the tertiary sector. As this shift occurs, grandparents and children no longer contribute to the economic well-being of the family but become economic liabilities. By the time children are old enough to bring in an income of their own, they are old enough to move out of the family home and start families of their own. This leaves the home setting without family care for the very young and the elderly.

The separation of work-home life came about gradually with men being the first to separate themselves from the home during work hours to work in factories. Urbanization, that is, people moving out of rural areas into city areas, combined with industrialization to split up the generations in terms of residence. It was, and still is, in urban areas where the jobs and housing are. Many elderly stayed behind in rural areas while their offspring migrated to the city. A city family became a nuclear family with two rather than three generations under one roof.

If mothers (and fathers) are not at home caring for their youngsters, where are the youngsters? In 1982, 17 percent of the care for young preschool age children was being provided by a grandparent; 26 percent of working mothers of children three to four were using group care. Family day care, that is, care in a private home where the children are not related, represents the most frequently used type of care facility. Day care centers providing for approximately 18 percent of American children are the most "visible" form of care; one-half of these centers cater to poor, usually single-parent families. Twenty-six percent of the children of working parents, as of 1982, were in an in-home care arrangement whereby a relative or nonrelative comes into the home or to which the child is taken. Of this group, 6 percent were cared for by sitters, nannies, or housekeepers. A high proportion of children needing day care, approximately one-third, are cared for in a multiple informal arrangement over the course of a single day.

Thus the institutionalization of health, child care, and elderly-ness is the present mode of care arrangement in this country. In 1978, for example, 38 percent of Medicaid expenditures went to institutions, whereas only 0.8 percent was expended on home health services. This mode has been criticized on various counts, including the lack of proper case management, low quality care, and poorly articulated and frequently contradictory goals of such care (Callahan and Wallack 1981). The restrictive nature of institutions and the inattention to maximizing possible functional independence for residents characterize such a setting as well.

Also swelling the size of the sandwich generation is a change in sex role stereotypes and the outcome of custody decisions. At once women are beginning to cluster in traditionally male occupations, traditional ways of looking at the roles men are assuming and should assume are being questioned, and more and more families are headed by a single parent. The shift is to assign a greater range and variety of roles and tasks to both the sexes and to increase the integration of these two role sets—family and work. Either in spite of this shift or because of it, more men are finding themselves single-parenting, assuming both work and family roles simultaneously with incumbent pressures to do both well. This trend in sex role stereotyping and outcomes of custody decisions in which men are assigned custody of children have been called a "significant" evolution in men's caregiving involvement (Bureau of National Affairs 1986: 18). Part of the evolution is the redefining of fatherhood, with fathers increasingly being depicted in ads for baby care and household products, attending parenting seminars, and the like. Furthermore, men are vocalizing their work-family dilemmas more openly. This has led industries to assume a greater awareness of the relationship between work and families, especially when top managers and executives are in this relationship. There is also a new emphasis on father participation at delivery and in childbirth classes, perhaps increasing the feeling of responsibility for the baby and its mother.

Men are beginning to share more in child care responsibilities with their wives, especially in families where at least one worker is a professional, according to a Catalyst (1986b) study. One father interviewed by the Catalyst group claimed that the greatest area of conflict in a two-career family is "deciding who's going to stay home when our son is sick" (1986b: 133). The urgency of one's work is now more frequently the determinant of who stays home with a sick child, rather than the assumption that it is the mother's "natural" role to do so.

Industry is beginning to respond to this change in sex role attitudes. The interest level of men in taking paternity leave and attitudes toward and interest in leaves are being monitored in some companies, further evidence that dependent care responsibilities may be shifting more to men. Based on these attitudes and interest, a paternal leave policy could be established with the possible effects of reducing the leave time taken by women. Sharing child care responsibility through maternity leave-taking can aid in the retention of "valuable" women employees as well.

Single-parenting is increasing for women as well, at a rate exceeding that of men. In 1986 one-quarter of all families with children were headed by a single parent and these single parents were mostly women (90 percent). What we are looking at is a growing number of employed women whose support of the family is entirely up to them. Between 1940 and 1983, for example, the number of families maintained by women nearly tripled (3,616 and 9,828, respectively).

Creation of the sandwich generation is the result of economic factors as well, and these factors combine with demographics to create the "nature" of this generation. Two of these factors are the inflation rate and cost-of-living level. There has been, and still is, much rhetoric about the need for families to have two income-earners in them. It is more than just coincidence, then, that there is covariance among women entering the labor force, the inflation rate, and the desire to maintain a certain standard of living we have come to expect. Jerome M. Rosow, president of the Work in America Institute, claims that wage slowdown and decline in real income have forced any available family member into the labor force (BNA 1986: 230).

The financial state and ensuing financial stress of many of the sandwich generation can be inferred from the definition of the sandwich generation. As noted earlier, these are people who are being depended upon by members of both the younger and older generations. Some of that dependency can be financial. Dana E. Friedman of the Conference Board and Family Information Center, a problem-solving and research facility in New York City, has stated it succinctly: "The [added] responsibility of an aged relative may come when the employee is also assuming the cost of child care or a college education."[7]

Working sandwich generation people are those whose financial futures are becoming more problematic as our population grows older, retires earlier, has fewer children, and draws more heavily on public resources. Social Security is a case in point, with some present recipients collecting three times as much in payments as the taxes they contributed to the program when they were working (Daniels 1988). This means that working members of the "baby boom" generation, as parents of a smaller child cohort who will someday work as well, will not be able to spread the burden of their retirement over as large a group of workers as the current retired population does. In 1975, 100 workers were supporting 30 Social Security recipients; in 2020, only 3 workers will be supporting them. Presently, each retiree is "supported" by 3.4 workers; retired baby boomers will be supported by only two workers.

Financial pressures as a result of being divorced, widowed, or married to someone who is making low wages have been attested to by some caregivers. The size of this group facing these pressures is unknown, but an estimate has it that 40 percent of working mothers are single, divorced, widowed, or married to men making less than $15,000 a year. The typical single mother, according to Bernstein (1989), earns only a bit more than $3 an hour.

A SANDWICH GENERATION OF WOMEN?

This book is about family relationships, family members as participants in the labor force, and what affects these relationships as well as labor force participation. Before we examine the reasons why women are pervasively the caregivers in society, let us look at how the family functions in society.

The family is society's most basic and pervasive institution. Its basic function, of course, is to propagate the human race. For far too many families, this is the point at which the family ceases to function. For most families, however, the next more important function is to rear children. Although many men are beginning to assume the child-rearing function, traditionally it has fallen to women. Historically and anthropologically, it has been men's prerogative to hunt and otherwise procure food for the family, whereas women's prerogative has been the preparation and storing of that food, a prerogative that keeps women homebound. Historically, it has been men whose labor for the family has taken place outside the home, whereas women's labor has taken place in the home. A large part of that labor has been child-rearing and nurturing. With women being present in the home more than men, other family functions have fallen to women: socializing the young into approved ways of behaving and preparing children for future social roles, for example.

This tradition of a family-task division of labor has persevered through-out the ages, perhaps but not necessarily because it functions so well, or at least has done so in the past. If it functions, it may be because men find it "easier" than women to assume the "heavier" tasks such as competing in the "market" for scarce resources; and perhaps it has been women's "easier" functions to child-rear and tend to domestic tasks.

This division of labor, for various reasons, has shifted in the home, however, with women entering the labor force and finding it difficult at the same time and in certain circumstances to carry out domestic tasks while working outside the home. As a result, the work-family role system has taken a new turn whereby the option for both sexes is to integrate roles in both work and the family in such a way as to best satisfy all members. If the facilitation of those roles is to be maximized, however, it is usually the women who must make the most adjustments—economic, social, and psychological. With this integration comes the inherent task of not allowing one role to adversely affect the other. To avoid adversity, women continue to assume, according to research on the subject (Pleck 1986), the lion's share of family responsibility in nurturing and caring for dependents, including those in the older generation.

How do we know that problems of the sandwich generation are, in the main, women's problems? Why is it that the focus is on women? Why is it that men seldom have to choose between working and caregiving, but women frequently do? And why is it that employment may significantly decrease the hours of assistance to parents by sons, but has no effect, or very little, on the assistance of daughters?

First, the volume of literature is replete with discourse on the effects of maternal, rather than paternal, employment on child care development, academic motivation and performance, and personality development (see Stuckey et al. 1982, for example). Next, we see that women are frequently heading households and so are in a potential caregiving circumstance. (We know that now one-fifth of our families are single-parent ones; 90 percent are maintained by women.)

Even though it may well be men's "nature" to be nurturing, it is usually the women who fall into what Sommers and Shields (1987) call the "compassion trap." Because of this, it is not surprising to find that most caregivers of the elderly are women. In a 1982 federal study reported on by Winfield (1987), it was discovered that 33 percent of a family's elder dependents were cared for by a daughter or daughter-in-law, whereas 17 percent were the responsibility of a son. A study reported by Myers (1988) revealed that parents are twice as likely to live with a daughter than a son and, although a daughter may enter the labor market during her caregiving years, the number of hours of assistance given to the elderly person does not decrease because of the daughter's employment. It may significantly decrease for a son, however. Dana Friedman of the Conference Board reports of a survey of employees of Travelers Corporation in which it was discovered that, even if it is the husband's mother who is the elder-dependent, it is usually women who are caring for her. An Aging Center representative at the University of Bridgeport (Connecticut) surveyed employees 40 years of age and older in three firms; they discovered that, of those giving eldercare, 80 percent were women. Employed women, it was discovered further, find family responsibility that goes with child care to be "most important."

Work accommodations being made to family matters is more a phenomenon of women than of men (Nieva 1985), with parenthood having different occupational consequences for women than it does for men. Women make major adjustments in their work lives to attend to family needs, whereas men are "pushed" further into their work activity and commitment by parenthood. The husband's attitude toward his wife working, the family's economic situation, and the number of children in the family help determine a women's labor force participation. Because of women's family roles, their intermittency of employment is affected also. Women, far more than men, give "taking care of the home" as the rationale for part-time work.

The August 1989 issue of *Ladies Home Journal* carried a lengthy article entitled "The Working Mom's Handbook: A Survival Guide to Help You Juggle Kids, Husband and Job—and Still Find Time for Yourself (well, a little)." The article points out that day care is not an option but a fact of life and, as a topic, needs to be addressed (by women) rather than rationalized. Working women interviewed for the article expressed concern over day care costs, quality and availability of day care as well as being working mothers and managing the family-work dilemma. Tips on what to look for in a day care center and on how to handle children's concerns regarding care centers are put forth in the article. The fact that the article focused on women and very little mention was made of their husbands has significance here.

An increasing argument is made for the legitimacy of a family career role for women. It holds that even though holding down a job outside the home has not been part of a woman's role set, it is more widely "accepted" if that job can be seen as an extension of her domestic role. Her outside-the-home role as a participant in the workforce is further legitimated if she has children, according to Hunt and Hunt (1982). Having children establishes normalcy to a working woman's situation since a woman caring for children is seen to be fulfilling her primary role—that of a caregiver. The physical as well as the emotional and psychological bind of caregiving at home and working falls to women rather than to men, in the main. Incumbent pressures of, even conflict between, the home-work relationship rest the heaviest on the women, so the argument goes.

EXPERIENCING DEPENDENT CAREGIVING: THE CONSEQUENCES

Being able to define the social and economic needs of members of the sandwich generation in the workforce will ultimately come from the determination of what they are experiencing—by an examination of the consequences of belonging to this generation and being members of the labor force at the same time. Effects vary as widely as human nature varies, of course, so we must examine what we believe to be the behavior of these people as it is generated by enacting the role of dependent caregiver.

First of all, dependent caregivers of the elderly may be involved in transporting the dependent to a variety of places such as banks, medical appointments, and the grocery store; housekeeping duties such as meal preparation, laundry, and cleaning may be other activities assumed by caregivers. Personal care and informal counseling account for part of the responsibility package. Legal and government agency assistance is commonly given by attendants of elders.

The two areas of legal assistance in which elders are the most needy are dealing with bureaucracies and the writing and signing of contracts. Services such as Social Security and supplemental security income payments, Medicare and Medicaid, military pensions, food stamps, social services, and nutritional programs are provided by administrative systems often too complex for an elderly person's capacities. Eligibility requirements are frequently spelled out incomprehensibly, computers as well as humans err, and rules and regulations for applying for assistance are often obscurely stated. The regulatory agencies and bureaucracies themselves are often insensitive to the needs and concerns of those they service (Barrow and Smith 1983). As a result an increasingly important family member function is to serve as mediator between bureaucracies and the aged (Hagestad 1986).

Not uncommonly, a legal contract such as a rent agreement can be written in small print, making it difficult to read. Securing appropriate and adequate legal advocacy to aid the expedition of such contracts, to write wills, to estate-plan, to protect against nursing home or other caretaker neglect and/or abuse are often the tasks of an elder person's caregiver.

"War stories" about caregiving responsibilities abound in the literature and in personal accounts. Various agencies, administrative bodies, corporations, university and college departments, and governmental agencies have undertaken studies to identify and evaluate these accounts.[8] The litany of dependent care consequences includes experiencing stress caused by being emotionally drained, worrying, using drugs, depression, anxiety, and health problems. The Department of Gerontology at the University of Bridgeport reported that 22 percent of the surveyed working caregivers were experiencing anxiety compared to only 8 percent of the noncaregivers who were employed. Those caring for Alzheimer and other brain-impaired victims and for the older elderly are particularly besieged (Stackel 1986–87). A Duke University study reported by Friedman (1986) informs us that in the general population only about 10 percent use drugs for depression and tension, whereas 33 percent of those caring for brain-disoriented dependents use drugs for these maladies. Employees caring for the very aged may suffer from the effects of caring for those with more serious and pernicious physical and/or mental conditions requiring a large financial outlay. One study discovered that in 25 percent of families with disabled elders, severe mental depression was present.

Dependent caregiving can rob energy as well. Typical is the personal account of the working woman, often the only daughter in the family, who winds up with the care of an infirm mother or father after she gets off work; the brothers "drop in" occasionally to check things out but refuse to offer help because their "lives are busy" (Landers 1989). In one case, the woman, married and with teenage children, not only spent most of her week time off-hours with her mother but weekends as well.

Financial problems, of course, may weigh heavily upon caregivers, especially those in lower paying jobs. Medicare and Medicaid benefits are limiting; for example, hospitalization for approved treatment under Medicare, as of January 1, 1989, requires $500 a year deductible for approved charges. Skilled nursing care, such as in a nursing home, is paid for only 20 days, providing nursing home care is an approved need. Medicare will cover up to 21 days of daily home health care by a skilled nurse, and intermittent care of up to 35 hours per week indefinitely.

Medicaid, which covers nearly 70 percent of nursing home residents, has increased the minimum which a couple must spend in order for it to kick in. Before January, 1989, this amount was $2,000; now it is $12,000. The spouse of a Medicaid nursing home resident is allowed to keep $815 per month of income for the nursing home spouse to remain qualified.

To evaluate the impact on work of these aforementioned outcomes and consequences, their relationship to work behavior is now examined. How do at-home-caused stress, depression, anxiety, and health problems, for example, affect work behavior and performance? Lateness and absenteeism, job leaving (turnover), reduced productivity, and lost work time spent tending to domestic responsibilities have been found to be linked to dependent care responsibilities. Feelings of being trapped between two sets of responsibilities and in a situation that one sees little reprieve from may be the basis of depression and related feelings. In 1984 members of the New York Business Group on Health Care were surveyed to determine the relationship between tardiness, absenteeism, decreasing productivity and using work time for personal reasons, and eldercare responsibilities. Not surprisingly, the two were found to be directly linked. Of the 69 respondents, two-thirds admitted to excessive use of the telephone at work for personal business on the part of caregiving employees, and nearly one-half reported a decrease in productivity among these employees. A large proportion of those members surveyed had noted signs of stress among caregiving employees.

According to Brazelton (1985), it is often painful and stressful for a working woman with a family to feel that she needs to do both well. When a woman is both a successful nurturer at home and has a successful career, she may feel split apart by having to set sometimes impossible goals for herself in both areas of activity. It is a three-way split for members of the sandwich generation, moreover.

Emotional ambivalence often exists for the working woman with children. There may be the feeling that unless she works, a woman is missing out on an important part of life and/or taking care of children is not rewarding work. For the working mother, there is always the possibility that she may sense the social bias against mothers who leave their babies in someone else's care; that it may not be alright to work and be a mother at the same time. Without reassurance that enacting two roles simultaneously is acceptable, working mothers are at the mercy of a society that takes little account of the importance of individual family needs. Then, too, to expect a woman to be equally successful in her work and at home adds responsibility upon responsibility. These expectations are stress-producers.

Another exploratory study of women caregivers in the labor force was funded by a grant to the National Association of Area Agencies on Aging. The agency making the study looked at caregiving among 77 women in Massachusetts. Among them, 36 had entered their present jobs with caregiving responsibilities already upon them. Over three-quarters admitted to experiencing conflict between work and caregiving demands, and nearly three-quarters claimed that these demands had increased since the onset of employment. Time pressures and worry were types of effects on work noted most frequently. More than one-third claimed to have had to make work adjustments in order to deal with domestic responsibilities.

Caregivers of Alzheimer's disease victims and victims of other brain-damaging ailments reported being especially hard hit. A survey conducted in San Francisco by the Family Survival Project revealed that an average of 9.3 hours a month were lost time for workers caring for people with these ailments.

Decreasing productivity has been cited as one result of the caregiving responsibilities on workers (see Stackel 1986–1987). The decrease is thought to be the result of lateness in coming to work, absenteeism, depression, stress, and time spent away from working on making non-work-related telephone calls.

SUMMARY

An awareness of and attention to the demographics of our present and future workforce should become the foundation upon which greater responsiveness to the family-work dilemma can be made. Attention to members of the sandwich generation is considered to be a vital issue of the 1990s because the size of this group is increasing and because many of these people are in the labor force already or will soon be joining it. Interest in and forward-thinking about these people need to grow in public and private sector industries, and should become an increasing part of the role of public policy setters.

Growth of this working dependent caregiver group is the result of an increasing labor force participation rate of women, the greatest increase taking place among women under 35 years of age with children under 3 years old. This growth has meant that there are fewer at-home care options available to dependent children and the elderly as well.

Yet another contribution to the swelling of this generation is the increase in the number of adult children who, for various reasons, are returning home, at least temporarily. We do not know exactly why they are doing so—a variety of social, economic, and psychological factors combine to produce this phenomenon—but the situation leaves those families in at least a quasi-dependency circumstance.

Kutner (1988) reports the "proportion of young adults who are being supported by their parents has reached a 30-year high." It is usually middle class and upper middle class families that are affected by the returning-home syndrome. Known as "boomerang kids," they return for another "bailout" by their parents. Some are not leaving at all until they marry, others stay at home because they cannot find affordable housing given their incomes, and still others have an unrealistic view of money, which gives them a distorted view of what it can do for them. This view is born out of the sometimes-called permissive 1960s era; they are caught in the backlash of liberal child-rearing. As one returner described by Kutner puts it: "I don't want to start at the bottom. I'm used to a certain way of life, and I don't like that I won't be able to buy what I want . . . [My parents have] always been there as a buffer. They've never let me fall hard."

NOTES

1. The survey questionnaire appears as Appendix A on page 153.

2. For discussion of this shift, refer to Herbert S. Parnes, *Peoplepower: Elements of Human Resource Policy*, 1984: 77, 78.

3. In 1920 approximately 27 percent of our labor force was in agricultural-mining jobs, 34 percent in manufacturing jobs, and 39 percent in tertiary sector jobs. In 1940 these proportions were 17 percent, 31 percent, and 45 percent, respectively; in 1984 the distribution was 2 percent, 30 percent, and 68 percent. Parnes projects that by 1990 over 72 percent of our workers will be in jobs in the tertiary sector.

4. John Naisbitt, *Megatrends*, 1984: Chapter 1.

5. The dependency ratio refers to a figure derived from dividing the number of people between the ages of 18 and 64 by the number of people younger and older than those ages, multiplied by a factor of 100. The result signifies the number of dependents every 100 "nondependents" must support.

6. However, an increase in the number of out-of-wedlock births is increasing the number of extended (four, even five) generation households.

7. "Eldercare: The Employee Benefit of the 1990s?" *Across the Board* 1986: 45.

8. Two such studies were conducted by the National Association of Area Agencies on Aging (NAAAA), and the New York Business Group on Health; see Janice L. Gibeau (1987) and Dana Friedman (1986) for details.

2

Industry Concern with Caregiving Employees

The sandwich generation is identified as are the consequences of membership; now it is fitting to assume that the consequences, in turn, affect the work life of those members who work in the formal labor force. The ways in which they affect workers and the responses that industries are, or should perhaps be, making and the rationale behind industry concern for the family-work dilemma are the subjects under scrutiny in this chapter. Such a rationale behind industry involvement and attentiveness to the social and economic needs of workers is based on the examination of the trend of "traditional" caregivers going into the workforce and then employing outside help for domestic duties, the aging of America, and fathers facing dependent care responsibilities with mothers entering the labor force. The need for more productive workers (Winfield 1987) and the inherent costs to employers of employees' work lives being affected by dependent care responsibilities are further rationales.

The idea that industries, both private and public, become involved in workers' private lives stems from U.S. employer practices generated in the late 1800s. "Welfare capitalism," "employee welfare," and "industrial paternalism" are terms applied to this involvement, and they refer to the role of business and government in the social lives of employees. Welfare capitalism was generated in the late nineteenth century along with the emergence of charity houses and public statutory provisions. It was created as a corporate response to lagging worker loyalty, possibly as a measure to neutralize worker militancy such as the kind associated with union activities, as a means to make workers more dependent upon business for essential services and, finally, as a public relations-building mechanism (Edwards 1979).

Industrial welfare was actually a type of social movement that peaked and then declined in intensity during the prosperous 1920s, the decline a result of growing employee resentment against industrial paternalism. Workers, in the beginning of the movement, were selected to receive recreational services, clinic and health care, pensions, stock sharing and other savings plans, and housing and educational benefits. U.S. Steel Corporation's 1902 stock subscription plan is a case in point. The corporation sold stock, at market price or usually a little less, to workers, with the firm paying a special premium on workers' shares for the first five years. In 1906 the firm adopted a job safety program, which reduced serious accidents by 40 percent. In 1910 the firm's workmen's compensation program was implemented as a measure to demonstrate that workers could gain something without contest and struggle. A pension plan was adopted the same year.

U.S. Steel was only one company adopting worker-betterment programs during this era, but such programs experienced demise as unions began to recognize them as a "thin veil spread over basic, unmet needs of . . . workers" (Edwards 1979: 96). Welfare capitalism was not addressing the perceived need for shorter working hours and the amelioration of oppressive work supervision. Corporations at this time began to scale down their programs, dismantle others, and shift the costs to the government through publicly financed benefits.[1] The government, after all, had the dollars, power, and authority to provide relief for workers.

Before World War II, employer benefit plans encompassing the welfare capitalism notion were practically nonexistent, a function of government's more aggressive posture in the field. However, since the war and especially since the 1960s, due to the growing dissatisfaction with government's performance in so many areas and the perceived limitations on what government is able to do effectively, the business sector is again taking up the case of welfare capitalism, albeit not to the extent nor in the manner that some proponents of dependent care policy would have it. To date, it is estimated that only about 200 employers offer eldercare assistance as part of their benefits packages (*The Wall Street Journal*, May 23, 1989). However, employee benefits packages generally constitute a growing proportion of compensation—the proportion increased 171 percent between 1969 and 1979, whereas wages and salaries increased 107 percent in this same period.

But government continues to play a relatively minor role in attending to workers' social needs. In the case of working mothers, for example, as if they were not here to stay, the U.S. government has provided relatively little support for its workers with dependent care needs, leaving a large share of that burden up to the individual employer. Other nations such as West Germany and Sweden are supportive of working parents' needs, whereas balancing child care and career in the United States is set against a backdrop of negativism toward working couples, according to Sandroff (1989). For all its economic growth and enhanced standard of living, the United States is alone among advanced industrialized countries in the lack of development of parental leave benefits. There is no national U.S. health insurance, no minimum maternity or parenting benefits, nor job-protected leaves at the time of childbirth or adoption. More than one hundred countries, including all the industrialized nations, guarantee workers some form and extent of job-protected, partially paid, maternity-related benefits. By 1968 nine European Community countries provided paid parental leave to both men and women. Other developed countries have implemented a coordinated set of public and private family policies, but the United States is "conspicuously" slow in responding to trends, according to the Bureau of National Affairs (1986).

Parental leave is a statutory right in most Western European countries such as Belgium, Denmark, France, West Germany, Italy, Luxembourg, and Portugal. It is usually unpaid leave lasting anywhere from 10 weeks to three years. Under normal conditions, the leave-taker has a right to his or her job upon return. Leave can be taken for the serious illness of a spouse, the death of a spouse and/or near relative, a child's wedding, a child's illness, or illness of the person caring for a child. (Portugal allows 30 days leave for the illness of a spouse.) Sweden has been especially attentive to family leave needs, and men, once not part of the family leave-taking picture, are increasingly taking advantage of leave privileges.

In Austria, workers may take from 16 to 52 weeks leave; 20 weeks may be paid, employees receiving 100 percent of their salaries. Canadian workers are allowed from 17 to 41 weeks leave, 15 of those weeks with 60 percent of salaries paid. In France, 18 weeks may be taken, with 90 percent of salary being paid for 16 weeks. In West Germany, 100 percent of salaries are paid from 14 to 19 weeks of the 14 to 26 weeks allowed for leave.

In Great Britain, the first maternity legislation was adopted in 1891. Although no cash benefits or job-reinstatement were part of the provision, women were prohibited from employment during the first four weeks following childbirth. The Beveridge Commission proposed a National Health Service in 1941, a comprehensive health care service providing free care to every woman. The proposal did not speak to job protection, however. Maternity-related benefits in the form of a small lump sum grant and an attendance and maternity allowance were established. The maternity allowance could be earned by women who worked and made national insurance contributions; the other two could be claimed on the basis of the husband's insurance record.

Under 1953 reforms, the payment period of maternity benefits—considered transitional welfare benefits—was extended to a period of 11 weeks before birth to seven weeks after. In 1974 maternity pay rights were again extended to include up to nine months of maternity leave to women who had at least one year of continuous service to one employer. Maternity pay lasted for four weeks; after four weeks a woman would be entitled to a flat rate allowance. The proposal met with protest from employers because of its cost, especially from smaller firms and those employing a large number of women, and on the grounds that it was not appropriate for the government to mandate employer-provided benefits.

A compromise plan adopted in 1975 stipulated that a woman must have worked on a full-time basis for the same employer for two years (five years' service for part-time work), allowed a maternity pay of 90 percent of "normal" earnings for six weeks, ensured job reinstatement and protection from unfair dismissal because of pregnancy.

Employer objections to the 1975 act were addressed in 1980 with the passage of the Employment Act. The act barred firms employing less than five people from holding job places for women on maternity leave if it was not reasonably impractical to do so, and in the case of a job not being held, a position not "substantially less favorable" could be offered.

The 1985 Social Security Act called for the integration of the various types of maternity-related benefits. With the "no-cost" constraint put on this integration (no cost meant that improvement in benefits for one group of women would be made at the "expense" of the benefits applying to another group), the conservative government was able to reduce the amount spent on maternity pay, thus reinforcing its stand on a reduction of government involvement in private lives. With this act, eligibility requirements were tightened, eliminating roughly 75,000 to 85,000 women from the maternity benefits program.

As of 1988, Statutory Maternity Pay (SMP) remains the primary maternity cash benefit. Basic benefits are at a flat rate and are paid directly to the woman by her employer, although SMP is fully funded from national insurance. In the case of an employee who has worked continuously for the same employer for two years, her entitlement equals 90 percent of her normal earnings and is made for six weeks, after which she reverts to the standard lower tier SMP level. A core period rule covers a woman with benefits in a 13-week period within an 18-week period before and after giving birth.

Other maternity benefits cover some women who do not qualify for SMP. These include a maternity allowance, a sickness benefit, a means-tested lump sum cash payment, and a job protection provision. These benefits cover all but a few workers. The plans take into account, to an extent, standards thought to be adequate for safe delivery and normal recovery, standards felt to reduce infant mortality and the incidence of low birth weight, and standards thought to reduce interrupted employment so harmful to a woman's economic security. Then, too, legal entitlements enabling women to maintain a continuous employment record have allowed women with heavy family obligations to fare better than those without guarantees (Stoiber 1989).

The cost burden to employees of these programs is thought to be minimal; the programs have been found to cause little concern to employers. The reasons for the minimum of burden are that eligibility standards are tight and, therefore, exclude nearly half of the female workforce, an employer can force a pregnant woman out of her job if she cannot perform up to standards, benefit levels are low, and because maternity pay is financed from social insurance funds, the cost is shared among all employers. (The concerns of employers most frequently mentioned are keeping the job open and finding a temporary replacement, and the failure of women to return to work after committing to do so.)

According to Pleck (1988), Sweden has the oldest and most generous paternity leave plan. The basic parent's benefits last for 180 days during the infant's first nine months, and workers are paid 90 percent of their salaries. The use of this leave is greatest among public sector employees. A special parent's benefit allows leave for 180 days to be used during the child's first four years. (Almost 28 percent of eligible parents used at least some of the special parent's benefit in 1980.)

As a temporary leave benefit, Sweden allows 60 days per child per year of paid leave to care for a sick child or to care for a child when the regular caregiver is unavailable. Fathers are entitled to a 10-day leave in connection with a mother's childbirth. Eighty-five percent of new fathers used at least some of this leave in 1981 for an average of 7.5 days. Variation in fathers' utilization of leaves takes place according to wives' earnings and education, marital status and age of the fathers, and employers' attitudes toward male employees who take these leaves. (Some employers may penalize male employees for taking leave under the "parental" rubric, indicating that infant-care leave policies may be gender-neutral in theory but not in practice.)

In the United States, use of paternity leave in the few large companies that allow it is minimal, according to Pleck (1988). Common practice is to put together a "leave package" that is made up of other paid and unpaid leave categories.

Do the demographics cited in the first chapter infer that there is a significant number of sandwich generation people in the workforce? The answer is, of course, yes. Confirming this assumption are findings from several studies that have shown the extent of sandwich generation workers in firms. Estimates of the proportion of employees of major corporations countrywide with eldercare responsibilities are as high as one-third. Keith Anderson, director of Corporate Communications at Pepsico, estimates that 20 percent of the workforce has eldercare responsibilities. Twenty percent of those workers over 30 years old owned up to dependent care responsibilities at the Travelers Corporation, according to Winfield (1987).

The extent of time spent on actual caregiving has been discovered in several studies. Dependent caregiving of workforce participants ranges from 3 1/2 hours a week to over 28 hours per week. In a study of employees of Travelers Corporation, of those surveyed (N = 739), 28 percent claimed to have spent approximately 10 hours a week in dependent care activities. Many "deadwood" employees are those overwhelmed by off-the-job problems. Employee assistance programs provide help (Odiorne 1987). By recognizing that many employees are facing family concerns and expenses, employers might see fit to examine such programs. Discovering the extent to which a firm's labor force is faced with such dilemmas is, of course, the first step toward an examination of an intervention program. This extent has been determined in many cases. In one study of 30 women executives, it was discovered that most of the single women faced eldercare responsibilities, and nearly all maintained that the family-career balancing act was a present concern or had been in the past (Collins 1988).

The age of dependent caregiving by labor force members is upon us. The bottom line is simply that there will continue to be an increasing number of members of the sandwich generation in the workforce to which industry should respond. This assertion can be deduced from such data as the following:

1. It is estimated that by the turn of the century, two-thirds of those hired will be women; it is women, as argued in the first chapter, who are most likely to be caregivers.

2. By this same time, three-quarters of all women between the ages of 45 and 60 will be labor force participants.

3. Hayghe (1986) has noted a fairly rapid increase in labor force participation of mothers with preschool-age children in the 1980s; nearly one-half of those mothers (with fathers present in the home) with infant children participated in the labor force in 1985, whereas only 31 percent were doing so 10 years earlier.

4. Lee (1987) observed that caregivers of frail elderly relatives represent a growing proportion of our labor pool.

5. An estimated 70 percent of the elderly rely mainly on relatives to meet long-term care needs (Callahan and Wallack 1981).

6. Twelve to 17 percent of the elderly have levels of disability so high as to be bedridden or require assistance in the most basic functions of daily living.

Labor force participation rates of men compared to women also foretell of a growing sandwich generation in the workforce. In 1960, 83.3 percent of the men 16 years and older were in the labor force; 77.9 percent were there in 1975; and 76.7 percent in 1985. Kamerman (1980) reports that since 1950 participation has decreased from 86 percent of the total men of working age to 76 percent. This will mean that employers will be drawing more from the labor pool of women than that of men. It is clear that women continuing to go into the workforce will mean that corporations will need to become more sensitized to family needs (Sullivan 1981).

Other demographics portend a shrinking supply of labor, giving industry another reason for looking into the dependent care needs of workers. A declining growth rate of the overall labor force and a smaller labor pool will mean that employers will have narrower and more limited choices of future employees. Between 1965 and 1980, the labor force grew at the rate of 2.2 percent each year, whereas it is projected to grow on average by about .8 percent from 1980 to the year 2000 (*World Develop-*

ment Report 1987). This is to say that future employees can afford to be more "choosy" about the firms they work for, and the competition among firms for employees will be heightened. In order to remain competitive, firms may have to heighten the "attractiveness" of jobs, including putting enhanced benefits in their compensation packages. Many studies showing an "idle" labor pool "out there" have been made, reinforcing the notion of making jobs more appealing to attract workers. One such study found that 26 percent of the unemployed mothers with children under five years of age would go to work if affordable child care were available. (Whether or not this labor is productive depends, of course, on a multitude of factors.) The point is that, with the impending labor shortage, some of this pool will need to be recruited to meet the labor demand. Making jobs attractive is one recruiting tool.

Winfield (1987) suggests that easy access to help for employees in times of crisis and during prolonged periods of the dependency of elders on workers will help maintain a corporation's competitive advantage and attract workers to jobs. Rosow (1986) argues that employers must recognize that home concerns will increasingly be raised at the workplace, concerns that represent a package of changes taking place, though slowly, in the workforce. The employee, thus, should not be considered property of management because no longer is there total devotion to work, exclusive of home concerns, except in a few instances. To address these changes, the competitive employer moves toward policy flexibility and freedom of choice for the worker. Flexibility and freedom of choice can be built into work-hour schedules, leave policies, and in support group activities held in the workplace, for example, according to Rosow.

CORRELATES OF HOME RESPONSIBILITY

Seen to correlate with responsibilities imposed upon working members of the sandwich generation are stress, job-leaving and absenteeism, deteriorating work performance and productivity, all of which affect, in turn, organizational effectiveness, the cost of doing business, the ability to compete, and corporate image. When these outcomes of the home-work dilemma are present, a company needs to look at its employee intervention program.

Wojahn (1988) sites lack of adequate child care as the basis of problems such as retention of workers, decreasing job performance, recruiting, and absenteeism, which all increase the cost of conducting business. Furthermore, working parents commonly must turn down promotions when work and home responsibilities clash, Wojahn found. Company management at Taylor Corporation, a printing business in North Mankato, Minnesota, recognizing the shortage of child care arrangements and that employees were turning down promotions because of it, started its own on-site child care center (Sandroff 1989). Levine (1984) reports from a survey that a personnel manager of a small consumer goods manufacturing firm said that the most frequent cause of absenteeism was complications with child care. According to Ellen Galinsky, the principal investigator of the (New York City) Bank Street College of Education survey, a company should intervene in an employee's personal life whenever job performance and productivity are being affected (Bureau of National Affairs 1986). What is needed are arrangements that allow men and women to function effectively at home and at work at the same time. Such arrangements lead to labor force stability. In the case of any plan, what must be weighed are the costs of reduced work hours and paid leaves of absence against turnover, absenteeism, and reduced productivity; the latter set of factors have proven to be the lighter. The cheapest and most efficient solution to these concerns, if we can call them that, is for management to become a "partner" in attending to employees' caregiving responsibilities. John E. Hayes, Jr., president and CEO of Southwestern Bell, maintained that it is a sound business decision to get involved with eldercare (Anderson-Ellis 1988).

Retirement Advisors of New York City conducted a corporate survey of managers indicating work and productivity problems relating to eldercare by employees (Creedon 1987: 22). Emotional stress was noted by over 50 percent of the respondents, whereas decreased productivity was observed by over 30 percent. The survey results not only indicated an awareness of workers' problems, but that attention to these workplace happenings had been given relatively little attention. Results of this same survey indicate that very few policies addressing these worker problems have been implemented among the 68 respondent companies surveyed (all in the greater New York area).

Yet another study shows awareness of workers' problems related to dependent care duties. In a study conducted by the chairman of John Hancock Financial Services and *Fortune Magazine*, 60 percent of the senior executives responding claimed awareness of specific work-related problems with elder caregiving employees (*Gazette Telegraph*, April 26, 1989). Forty-five percent had noticed employee stress; 38 percent noticed late arrivals and early departures; 30 percent noticed absenteeism among caregiving employees. In this case, the chairman, E. James Morton, was prompted to urge the discovery of humane solutions to the eldercare "problem" experienced by employees.

An increasing rise in the number of single-parent households and its results—more people facing additional financial strain—also exacerbates the dependent care problem for employees. Financial strain almost can be assumed in single-parent families. One-half of all families maintained by the mother alone now live below the poverty level. In 1980 more than 20 percent of all households with children under 19 years old were single-parent situations. Mothers increasingly become heads of households as the rate of children born out of wedlock and the divorce rate increase. As a matter of fact, the number of working mother heads-of-households more than doubled between 1970 and 1985. It has been forecast that 67 percent of the children born in 1984 can expect to live in a one-parent household for some portion of their lives.

But many companies deny that dependent care issues are workforce issues and suffer because of this denial, in spite of the evidence indicating employer assistance to working caregivers results in higher employee morale, lower turnover and absenteeism, increased productivity, and lower operating costs. "Companies are finding that if they're not family-friendly, they're losing employees," so states Lorraine Dusky (*Gazette Telegraph*, October 15, 1989). A family-friendly company, one that accommodates the personal, social, and economic needs of employees, is one that retains valuable and productive workers. However, it is often considered "wimpish" for a company to be family-friendly (e.g., offering child care assistance), according to Kris Rondeau who organized the 3,500-member Union of Clerical and Technical Workers in 1988 in Cambridge, Massachusetts (Sandroff 1989). But in this case, management was led to care about family issues among employees when it became known that there was a shortage of clerical workers in Cambridge. The union's family policy package includes $50,000 a year in child care stipends to defray assistance costs.

The cost of turnover and absenteeism as a result of companies failing to accommodate the family needs of workers—to be family-friendly—is the issue here. It has been estimated that businesses lose $3 billion dollars each year due to employees missing work to deal with child-related problems (*Gazette Telegraph*, October 1, 1989). In contrast, the Union Bank in Los Angeles discovered that for every $3 spent in aiding employees in some form or another, $4 were "saved" in reduced absenteeism and turnover, and increased productivity. Aetna Life and Casualty determined that the costs of recruiting and training to fill a vacancy, plus lost productivity, amounted to 93 percent of the first-year salary for the position (Sandroff 1989).

JOB-LEAVING

One of the possible effects of the work-family strain is job-leaving. Among 150 caregiving families of the elderly, interviewed for a study done at the Philadelphia Geriatric Center, it was discovered that over one-quarter of the then nonworking women had left the labor force to care for their mothers; another 26 percent of those still working had entertained the notion of quitting or, at least, cutting back on the hours they would work (Winfield 1987). Creedon (1987) notes that 11.6 percent of all caregiving daughters had left their employment because of caregiving.

The implication is that job-leaving may often spell the loss of pension benefits—a tab society may have to pick up (Azernoff and Scharlach 1988). As a matter of fact, what employers are doing in their firms vis-à-vis employees' work-family bind may be driven by interest in reducing the burden of dependent care on the taxpaying public, so aver Kamerman and Kahn (1987).

Aetna Life and Casualty Company's family leave policy, adopted in 1988, may be just a case in point. When the policy was adopted, managers and corporate officers were informed that 21 percent of the women who had left technical positions had done so because of family responsibilities. In a study of the no-longer-employed in the San Francisco area, it was discovered that 22 percent had left their jobs to care for brain-impaired victims such as those suffering from Alzheimer's disease. Such "victims," by virtue of the longevity of their illness, often become the recipients of public policy and burdens to taxpayers. The debilitating effects of Alzheimer's disease are well documented: decreasing brain function, vision, and bladder control, possible deafness, the possible need for oxygen, a myraid of medications and surgery, all predict a long illness and the eventuality of "going public" for one's assistance needs.

A survey conducted in 1986 at Corning Glass Works in upstate New York revealed that women employees were twice as likely to quit their jobs as men. One job-leaver, a senior level manager, was regarded as having "great potential" for the company (Ehrlich 1989). Replacing these women, company officials estimated, costs more than two million dollars a year. The company now offers salaried employees the option of working part-time with flexible hours.

Further evidence that family assistance plans aid in retaining workers was found with the Campbell Soup Company. One of the reasons people went to work for the company in Camden, New Jersey, was because of its subsidized on-site day care center for 125 employee children. The center came about after many luncheons with small groups of employees to invite suggestions. James H. Moran, director of public relations, called the center a good way to attract and keep the best talent (Sandroff 1989).

Accommodating family needs to keep valuable employees at work—those who know complex procedures, for example—even on a part-time, scaled-back flexible schedule costs a firm less than hiring an inexperienced worker and makes it hard for competitors to "steal" them away from the family-friendly company.

Inflexible work rules, in contrast, are the major reason that many people leave big corporations. Even so, it is possible to reach CEOs who are resistant to change. Arguments for a flexible work schedule need to be presented in a nonconfrontational manner. Such tactics as pointing out that flexible working hours are allowed to other employees in different positions, remaining firm in one's stand, and "going around" the problem frequently produce the desired results "for companies are changing swiftly these days" (Sandroff 1989: 197) and are willing to compromise.

Flextime as an inducement to retain a job-holder was suggested by an Aetna manager who said she preferred to retain a good worker who works only 32 hours a week than train a new one who would work 40 hours a week (Trost 1989). Business loses with the loss of employees who are difficult to replace and/or who are at their peak of productivity. Younger middle age women (from 35 to 44 years old) are most likely to be honing their job skills and training and gaining experience that will help them maximize their productivity. At the same time, these people may be facing increasing dependent care responsibilities, some so divisive concerning their commitment to work that job-leaving may be the result.

This scenario of job-leaving translates into growing pressure on the workplace and affects business' bottom line. The notion of providing parental leave, for example, as a good business practice was reinforced by those at Catalyst (1986b) who investigated such leave among large U.S. firms. Parental leave gives a firm a "clear-cut advantage" in recruiting intelligent, capable, and productive people to one's labor pool. This proactive stance can give business clients the message that the company's policymakers are competent, and can enhance company image. Another Catalyst study (1986a) found that some companies were modifying their parental leave policies to keep pace with other firms, to attract new employees, and to respond to the increasing number of employees, especially managers, who were requesting leave.

Some employers who shy away from allowing parental leave, notably the leave of mothers, sometimes do so in response to the myth that leave-taking mothers are not likely to return to the workplace. A national magazine reported a tendency to return, and to do so sooner, to the workplace among women who work for companies that have a parental leave policy than among those who work for firms that do not. A 1987 *Fortune* 500 company discovered that, before a child care and support system to reduce stress was instituted, 25 percent of its women workers quit after taking maternity leave; only 2 percent quit after the new policy was implemented.

Managers also may be particularly resistant to part-time work schedules, regarding the traditional 40-hour work week as "sacred" and denying that anyone working fewer hours does anything useful (Rodgers and Rodgers 1989). Managing the work of leave-takers and part-timers can be of concern to those companies that offer dependent care assistance. But such concerns can be addressed. For example, if shifting work from one employee to another is a problem when tasks are highly specialized, cross training employees may ease the concern. Maintaining healthy client relationships is eased by anticipating the leave, coordinating the work left by the leave-taker and part-timer, and applying teamwork.

Managers should ask their employees about family needs (Sandroff 1989) in order to adequately prepare for possible contingencies (e.g., pregnancy). These contingencies are no longer rare occurrences because they increasingly impinge upon a larger proportion of the workforce. As common occurrences, then, employers should look upon child care assistance as another benefit like medical insurance and vacations, not to be singled out and used to label employees as "requiring special treatment," and therefore high risk. Managers who are this flexible can help their companies "ride the waves of changes" taking place in the workplace (Sandroff 1989: 197).

The response of small businesses to child care responsibilities in the form of leave policies is especially important to consider because small firms employ approximately 50 percent of the U.S. workforce, create the most jobs (earnings from small firms account for about 40 percent of the GNP), and employ a large number of women (Butler and Wasserman 1988). The attitude of the small firm is important also from the standpoint of recruitment; the benefits a business offers is directly related to its ability to recruit quality employees.

Small business employer attitudes toward worker benefits were revealed in a study conducted by Butler and Wasserman (1988). Despite the uniqueness of each situation, many small businesses adopted employee benefits policies because it was in their own best interests to do so. The cost of replacing a high caliber employee was the main consideration. (The "generosity" of the policy varied by the extent to which the business owners valued family concerns, however.)

Small businesses have three main areas of concern about leave policies. One of these is financial (the other two being operational, and client-oriented). The financial concern involves doubling up on salary—one for the leave-taker and the other for the replacement. In the case of unpaid leave, the costs involve continuation of contributions toward employee benefits, and the possible loss incurred through lower productivity of the replacement. The replacement's salary may be offset, however, by the fact that a productive employee who is not granted leave may quit, meaning that a new worker has to be recruited and trained. In the case of paid leaves, employer-employee contributions to an insurance plan usually finance such leaves.

Going part-time may be an alternative to leaving entirely, but that is often a signal to the employer that the employee is not on the "A team," a situation that may relegate women especially to the fringes of power in an organization. Implied is that a part-time employee will not be as serious about work as those on an "all-or-nothing" track.

Distinguishing women workers from men workers through maternity leave-granting and other means can contribute to the notion that women are marginal workers with special frailties, whose labor force participation is at best temporary. Of course, it is usually women and not men who take advantage of disability policies, a fact that may discourage some employers from hiring women, although men are also allowed disability leave in many cases.

According to several articles (see Ehrlich 1989, for example), family-career women are valuable assets to a firm. They make ideal middle managers, and middle management is a "proving ground" for the top management level (Kantrowitz et al. 1989). Any efforts by a company toward maintaining women in these positions is a step toward retaining often talented and already and potentially valuable employees. With a labor shortage looming, this is an important point.

But the costs of retaining women often are an issue to companies. However, Sandroff (1989) found that women cost companies only slightly more than men in total time lost due to illness, accidents, and maternity leave-taking combined. (The average number of days lost annually for men was 2.8 and for women, 3.4, or slightly more than half a day.) Women, of course, may be more "costly" to the company during child-bearing years, but men are usually more costly later on: For every woman who will have a heart attack, nearly five men will do so, according to Sandroff's study. The ratio for alcohol abuse is 1 to 2, respectively.

It is often difficult for both employers and employees to acknowledge the conflict between home and work situations. The problems of keeping up a family-work connection are often masked by employees' reluctance to express their feelings for fear of hurting their careers. This is particularly true of women, but it is becoming more true of men as well. In a *Business Week* article (March 20, 1989) Richard Belous, an economist at the National Planning Association, was quoted as saying that being on ". . . the mommy track is like a millstone around your neck. CEOs and rain-makers don't come out of the mommy track" (Ehrlich 1989). Expressing family-work concerns may be part of the millstone.

Even when employees ask for assistance with behavioral and/or emotional difficulties, their requests may only "represent the tip of the iceberg" of dependent care-related stress, observes Elaine Cohen of Pathfinders, a counseling service in Scarsdale, New York. She found that for every six requests for assistance, there are 60 employees taking part in a dependent care workshop at their places of employment.

Industry also gets involved with working sandwich generation members because of the preferred and traditional mode of caring for the elderly—in home-based care. Only about 5 percent of the elderly and other dependents in the United States live in nursing homes, attesting to the preference for home-based care, often called the "maiden aunt" tradition. The alternatives are intermediate independent living for the relatively self-sufficient and, for those not self-sufficient, a nursing home facility. The nursing home is usually regarded as a last resort for those who have exhausted all other care possibilities.

There are basically two kinds of nursing homes: skilled nursing facilities in which the residents require and receive convalescent care, and care for chronic illnesses on a continuous daily basis. Intermediate care facilities are for residents not experiencing medical distress or crisis but who require help with such functions as walking, dressing, and eating. Presently, the average stay in a nursing home is two to three years. Medicaid benefits vary by state, and are allowed (as of January 1989) to those who are living at or below 85 percent of the federal poverty level ($5,770 for a single person in 1988). For those residents who live beyond the months covered by Medicare, the remainder of their stay in a nursing home must be paid for out of someone's pocket. The only alternative may be home care by a family member, unless the dependent wishes to spend his or her assets down to $7,000. In that case, Medicaid will pick up the tab for nursing home care. (The American Health Care Association's estimate of the percentage of nursing home residents who pay their bills out-of-pocket is only 30 percent.) But the Medicare system is in trouble. Like Social Security, Medicare has a trust fund that pays for hospital and short nursing home stays. Surpluses from the Medicare fund are lent to the Treasury. But unlike Social Security, Medicare's Hospital Insurance fund will run out of money by the year 2005, according to Garland (1990). Because of soaring health costs and growth in the number of elderly people, the fund is projected to pay out more than it is taking in starting in 1998. (Social Security Commissioner Robert M. Ball advocates transferring part of the Social Security tax to finance the faltering Medicare fund. This transfer would pay for Medicare until 2020.) It is estimated that Medicare will sustain a $27.3 billion deficit by the turn of the century. Federal legislation on long-term and home care has not been enacted as of October, 1989 (but it is pending in the 101st Congress). Services to the elderly have diminished and competition among health care providers has increased the price of these services.

Industry may also become involved in the dependent care needs of employees because of the burden—both financial and psychological—of caring for someone on a long-term basis. Long-term care involves a great financial, social, and psychological investment by the caregiver, and caregivers often do not have the resources to pay for out-of-home care for dependents. With the average cost of a nursing home, in 1975, at $7,300 a year, and 68 percent of the disabled, 73 percent of the disabled elderly, and 76 percent of the institutionalized with household incomes of less than $7,000 a year, the case can be made for some outside financial help. Medicaid pays for only 28 to 31 percent of all long-term care services and 51 percent of all nursing home care. It is not surprising, then, to find that, in 1976, from 38 to 44 percent of total national spending for all long-term care was paid directly by consumers out-of-pocket.[2]

PRODUCTIVITY

One of the most important reasons, from an industry standpoint, for companies to respond to the dependent care needs of workers is productivity. Many elements comprise productivity, the human element being the basis upon which all others function.

An increasing interest in worker productivity and human resource enhancement can be noted in the literature, both "popular" and academic, of the past few years, and in other media such as video tapes. Enhancing human capital to stem the tide of decline in U.S. productivity rate seems to have become a crisis issue.

The link between productivity and problems at home is clear. Because productivity is related to job performance and work and family life are integrated, according to Sullivan (1981), what happens at home affects a worker's productivity. Therefore, there is a need for a policy that promotes a higher level of integration of work patterns and corporate life, and family life-styles. This higher level should provide a basis for greater personal and family security, which, in turn, should be a basis for greater productivity, according to Sullivan.

The growing concern over productivity stems from the decreasing rate of GNP per capita in the United States. From 1947 to 1973, the average annual growth rate was 3 percent, but it has not been that high since 1974. In the service sector, the sector in which over 70 percent of U.S. workers are employed, output per worker is growing at less than .6 percent a year (*World Development Report* 1988).

The virtues of increasing productivity have been described at length. Patton (1983) notes that increased productivity rewards the business in which it occurs, as well as its stockholders, the community, and workers, plus employees who are hired as a new productive capacity is added or whose jobs are revitalized. With increased productivity, competitiveness is maintained and inflation combatted because profits increase.[3] This profit, less worker salaries, is used to pay for other costs of doing business. Enhancing the value of the product, then, becomes the goal of a firm, value-enhancement coming from more and better input into the work effort on the part of employees. More and better input is what higher productivity is all about.

Productivity leads us to an examination of the relationship between technology and human capital. Technology in and of itself has no value. It has value only when the human factor is applied to it. Ideas and skills are embodied in technology, which is, first of all, a product of human capital effort. Technology does not increase productivity; the productivity of labor does. If a company wants productivity to increase and, thus, the profit margin, it must treat its workers as its most important asset. As Odiorne (1987: 169) puts it: "The level of productivity of a worker is very possibly under the control of the worker and not some natural law."

In the strictest sense, productivity refers to the ratio between worker output—ideas, some outcome—and a measure of worker input such as person-hours of work. To change that ratio, then, our attention should be directed at enhancing the *quality* of labor input per person-hour of work, as that work is applied to technology.

But certain factors stand in the way of enhancing the quality as well as quantity of labor input, however. Most of these factors refer to the "failings" of physical capital, and to absenteeism, turnover, and level of job satisfaction. As noted, the mental-emotional separation between the workplace and the home has often been blamed for absenteeism, turnover, and tardiness, all factors that affect productivity. And despite claims to the contrary, there probably are valid reasons to assume that attending to workers' social needs could improve productivity by reducing the incidence of these "failing" factors (Miller 1984).

Four techniques to improve America's workforce through increasing productivity are generally acknowledged. The first is to increase the amount of physical capital—technology—with which workers can interact. The second and third are to shift workers out of less productive sectors of the economy into the tertiary/service sector where there is the greatest potential to maximize their marginal product, and to better manage these workers. The fourth technique speaks directly to the issue at hand—to make qualitative improvements in the human factor of production.

To illustrate this fourth point, let us consider the preindustrial work world. In agriculture, where most work was done, farmers produced just enough to maintain the family, plus a small surplus to trade. What was not consumed or traded essentially was wasted produce. Therefore, any effort to produce over and above what was needed to sustain the family and to trade was, in effect, wasted effort. The producer, therefore, had no incentive to work harder than necessary to produce what was immediately needed.

In the industrialized workplace, at least where work is done for someone else, workers labor to produce more than what can be "sold" (exchanged) for the amount needed to cover the fixed and variable costs of doing business—contractual obligations such as rent, selling, administrative, and utilities costs, the costs of materials of production, and wages and salaries. Because there are fixed and variable costs, the ability or potential to have something "left over" to comprise profit is a matter of worker productivity. The simplifed hypothetical situation becomes this: the greater the productivity, the greater the "sales" and, therefore, the greater the ability to increase a firm's profits.

The input of automation must be considered when discussing productivity. Obtaining greater output with the same amount of labor input and making the labor process easier are the aims of automation. It makes for greater ease of labor as well as for greater and more efficient productivity.[4] Several schools of thought speak to the pursuit of productivity through automation (but not necessarily to making labor easier). One school of thought is associated with the "scientific management" of labor. The scientific management concept is attributed to Frederick W. Taylor, an American engineer and consultant who became the leading advocate of time-and-motion studies (Watson 1987). Although Taylor regarded the worker as merely another tool in the productive process, his method, when applied, did result in greater productivity for the company. Another mechanism of Taylorism was to break down jobs into smaller components, thus increasing occupational specialization (the division of labor). This had the effect of complicating record keeping and supervisory and worker training tasks, an effect that may ultimately outweigh the gains in productivity (Macarov 1982).

Taylorism, with its lack of acknowledgement for workers' feelings, desires, and interrelationships, led to the Human Relations school of thought about productivity. This school emphasized the importance of changing the physical conditions of work—lengthening rest periods and shortening work time, for example—to take into account worker feelings and job satisfaction.

The Structuralist school of thought on productivity takes as its premise that workers must have job satisfaction in order to be productive. Satisfaction comes about by job redesign based on worker preferences. Worker participation in the planning for redesign and in the decision-making process are inherent to this school, which in today's firms has taken the form of quality circles and networking among and within levels of a company's authority structure. Greater worker autonomy is often achieved through greater decision-making participation. Greater recognition of workers as contributors to the organization can be considered as part of this school of thought as well.

Much has been written about what affects work orientation, or what affects a person's view of the work he or she is doing, which may in all likelihood affect productivity (Watson 1987). Work orientation is itself affected by the cultural underpinnings of work. A culture is a system of shared meanings, attitudes, values, and behavior patterns by members of a group. The meanings that people assign, in a sense, reflect their values and attitudes about "proper" behavior and thinking. Human existence and behavior are defined and driven by culture.

For centuries, human cultures have defined working as good and virtuous, as a way of serving God. To work well is a way to turn one's back on the mundane and move upward toward virtue and other-worldliness. Industrial capitalism spawned the view that personal and social advancement is gained by hard and effective work; not working is viewed as being a failure in and a disgrace to society.

Work has other meanings as well. It has both an expressive (intrinsic) meaning and an instrumental (extrinsic) meaning, which reflect cultural parameters and infer different approaches that people take to work. Expressive and instrumental elements both can motivate productivity. Meanings attached to work can be placed on a continuum from intrinsic/expressive to extrinsic/instrumental (Watson 1987).[5] An intrinsic orientation suggests that the employee finds work to be an enriching personal experience and a challenge, a means by which an individual finds self-fulfillment. An extrinsic orientation suggests that work yields no value in and of itself but is merely a means to an end, that end being a paycheck. In this orientation, self-fulfillment is sought outside of work.

These work orientations demonstrate that work and its output are a function of the particular meanings that people attach to them and to the motivations to work as well—the work itself. Meanings, orientations, and motivations can be affected by "incentives" offered to work—wages, salaries, benefits, agreeable social and physical working environments, available technology, the chances for upward mobility—and the *nature* of the incentives themselves. It is often the case that when one of these incentives is not adequate, the others seem inadequate as well. What follows can be loss of incentive to maximize productivity.[6]

The idea of a direct relationship between worker satisfaction and productivity underlies the great majority of studies in this area during the past 50 years (Macarov 1982). Problems associated with these studies, however, make the existence of this relationship seem doubtful at best. Some of these problems concern the fact that usually only "successful" case studies get into print, that the relationship between the two variables may be spurious, and that increased incentives may not lead to increased productivity. Motivations sometimes conflict, making it difficult to identify what actually motivates greater productivity. There is the difficulty of quantifying motivation and the weakness of replicating motivation studies. Also, the work setting—industrial or tertiary—often determines whether the emphasis should be on quantity or quality. In an industrial setting, the emphasis falls on the former; in service industries, emphasis is on the latter. However, it is Scanlan's (1976) conclusion that if there is a high degree of job satisfaction, there is more likely to be high rather than low productivity.

Companies in which dependent care programs are part of the benefits package report positive results. Improved morale, reduced absenteeism and turnover, and improved productivity were reported by the Indiana firms of Nyloncraft in Mishawaka, and Lincoln National Life Insurance of Fort Wayne, as well as the First National Bank of Atlanta (a consortium of firms with dependent care programs), and Hoffman-LaRoche, Inc. of Nutley, New Jersey (Peterson and Massengell 1988).

Senator Christopher Dodd (D-CT), one of the original sponsors of an early parental leave bill, argued that parental leave as part of a company's benefits package would reduce absenteeism, thus saving the company money, and would further allow a firm to more accurately plan for vacancies due to leave-taking.

In a study of 415 companies with child care programs, nine-tenths of those reporting on company image claimed improvements in public relations and over half reported a positive effect on productivity and the reduction of absenteeism. Nearly two-thirds attributed some reduction in turnover to their programs, and 80 percent reported gains in recruitment in such fields as high technology, assembly work, and computer programming.

Flextime is more and more identified as a means to reduce stress caused by the home-work dilemma, and thus increases productivity. Nollen (1979) tries to answer the question: Does flextime improve productivity? From case studies of over 10,000 workers and 500 supervisors in eight surveys (covering such businesses as pharmaceuticals, banks, insurance, transportation, utilities, and government agencies), Nollen found that 48 percent of the case studies reported a gain in productivity. (In both cases, supervisors were less likely to report gains than workers.) Increased productivity was identified because of greater work effectiveness, enhanced work quality and quantity, greater work performance output both daily and annually, and better completion of daily work requirements. Productivity increases may have been the result, too, of the better work organization, of tasks more efficiently allocated, of meetings, visits, and telephone calls being concentrated into shorter time periods, and work requiring concentration being done more effectively before or after a core working period when there are not as many interruptions. People also have different biological "clocks," making them more effective either early in the morning or late in the afternoon, and flextime can accommodate these differences.

Concerning the productivity of part-time workers, sometimes thought to be hard to determine, studies noted by Rodgers and Rodgers (1989) indicate that the productivity of part-timers is, in certain cases better than the productivity of their full-time counterparts, and in all cases no worse. One study showed that, hour for hour, part-time employees carried greater caseloads and serviced them with more attention. In terms of career opportunities for part-time employees, sometimes felt to be not deserving of consideration, it takes "a lot of ingenuity and cultural adaptability to devise meaningful part-time work opportunities." (Rodgers and Rodgers 1989: 127). In this regard, fast-track career progress on notions and implementation may need modification. Certainly, there should be less tendency to equate productivity with the hours spent at work; hard work does not necessarily translate into greater productivity.

Zigler and Frank (1988) acknowledge that the availability of dependent care options acts to "encourage" employees whose role as worker is increasingly at odds with the caregiving role. Firms with these options that integrate the work and home spheres, are finding an increase in worker output and allegiance, and a decrease in attrition. Such an integration eases stress and frees workers' energies for their jobs, thus increasing the likelihood of productivity.

Another valid argument for attention to dependent care needs of workers, especially those having to do with children and young adults, relates to quality of life and life-styles. No one needs to be reminded that the burden of the future lies in the hands of children to a great extent. They are human resources and potential contributors to the workforce and, thus, to its level of economic growth. How "healthy" they are emotionally, physically, mentally, and socially depends to some extent at least on the quality of life they experience as they grow. Some groups of children in society, as well as adults, are being deprived of the quality of life that would afford them a healthy social, mental, and physical development. With this deprivation, how can they maximize their future "contribution" to society?

Poverty and deprivation can be defined in several ways. "Being poor and deprived" usually refers to one's economic status. But poverty must also be regarded from a social standpoint. There are many levels and kinds of poverty: social, psychological, physical, and mental. There is also relative and absolute poverty. The kinds of poverty are all relative to how other groups in society experience them.

Some children are deprived of the opportunity to develop healthy social, mental, and physical lives, compared to other groups, such as the elderly, for instance. Children are becoming "less equal" as our elderly population grows.[7]

Preston (1984) argues that a rapidly growing elderly population has disadvantaged, and will continue to disadvantage, children. He compares income levels of families, over time, to determine the changes in numbers living below the poverty level. In 1970 the incidence of poverty among elderly people was double the national average; by 1982 the incidence had dropped *below* the national average. In 1970 the incidence of poverty among children was 37 percent less than in 1982; in 1982 it was 56 percent greater than it was among the elderly. The young-elderly, those between 55 and 64, experienced a net worth increase of 34 percent between 1977 and 1983, whereas those 70 to 74 experienced a 74 percent increase.

According to Weicher (1989), it is younger adults who are experiencing a decline in wealth and who, because of this, could have the greatest need for assistance to maintain desirable life-styles and quality of life. Weicher reports that from 1977 to 1983 household heads under 25 years old suffered the greatest decline in mean net worth, a decline of 37 percent. Younger adults obviously cannot afford the life-style their parents enjoyed at a younger age. Interest rates and prices take a larger proportion of young adults' incomes today than when their parents were young.

A comparison of federal spending on the elderly and children also shows how children are being disadvantaged. In 1984 the amount of federal expenditure on children represented only one-sixth of the amount spent on the elderly.

Preston regards the family as the main source of support of children, and increasingly less support contributes to the disadvantage of children. He points to the "disappearing act" of fathers as the main cause of the decrease in support. In 1960 only 5.3 percent of births were out of wedlock (a situation that assumes the father takes no substantial responsibility for the child). Over 18 percent of births in 1980 were out of wedlock. Furthermore, of those children born in wedlock between 1977 and 1979, 43 percent can expect to live in a "disrupted" family situation by the time they are 16 years old; the figure for 1963 to 1965 was 22 percent. The likelihood of fathers making child support payments is grim. In 1978 only about 40 percent of children living with their mothers (without the fathers present) received child support from their fathers.

Expansion of Social Security benefits in the 1970s accounts for much of the poverty reduction among the elderly, and thus their "advantage" over young people. An increase in the incidence of poverty among children can be attributed to an increase in the number of females heading households. This increase came about in spite of the fact that mothers were entering the labor force at an increasing rate and, by doing so, contributing to an increase in family income. But increases in family income by virtue of women working must be seen in light of the expenses incurred—child care, travel, clothes, meals, and such.

DEMOGRAPHICS, SOCIAL CHANGE, AND INDUSTRY

It is readily apparent that policy in the United States may not be keeping up with the changing demographics, and the private sector may be well advised to take up the slack. Increasing longevity is recognized but barely and inadequately accommodated by Medicare and Medicaid. We are keeping people alive and well longer, and take pride in being able to do so, but society has not attended well to the spinoff of longevity. As people live longer, the chances of being physically and/or mentally disabled with pernicious illness and disease increase. We see the elderly living to be old-old, frequently using up their life savings to sustain a quality of life they have worked hard for, but being reduced to penury in spite of their best efforts to provide for the future. Even foresightedness cannot accommodate, in many circumstances, long-term and debilitating illness. Yet old-old people comprise the fastest growing elderly group in our society and those most likely to experience debilitating illness.

Levine (1984) maintains that our changing demographics have created a need for employers to consider employees' child care problems and their affect on productivity. It is assumed, and safely so, that there is a problem in this regard. If not, we would not see so much literature on the subject, nor the public policy efforts being made in this direction, nor the number of studies conducted by both private and public organizations, agencies, and businesses, which seek to determine the extent and nature of the problem. Some studies have led to action.

In light of future labor shortage and changing demographics, employers are being urged to "revolutionize" their workforces.[8] Various ways are being tested, such as giving workers better training, raising wages, intensifying recruiting, and hiring older workers. Firms might begin to think of hiring "older" people as temporaries, full-time, and part-time workers. Not only would firms benefit from older workers' strong work ethic, knowledge, and experience, but families of these older workers would be eased of the financial strain often incurred by a dependency situation.

Crawford (1990) states that older workers are becoming more attractive as corporations seek to cut costs in the face of increasing competition at home and abroad. Hiring older people, once considered unorthodox, is becoming routine and makes good business sense as they earn less than comparable full-time employees, and many part-time jobs do not provide expensive fringe benefits. Retirees can also be used to train younger workers.

Firms are beginning to take advantage of this available labor pool. Aerospace Corporation of Southern California has devised a program called "casual employment." The company hires back some of its retired workforce with the rationale that these workers with highly marketable skills might take their skills and go to work for someone else. Out of 100 or so workers who retire each year, Aerospace hires back 20 to 30 on a part-time basis. The Bureau of Labor Statistics reports that workers 55 and older accounted for 9.7 percent of all temporary workers in 1989. Temps and Company, a national personnel services company, found that retirees represent the fastest growing portion of its workforce. MSI International, a personnel services firm, estimates that 15 percent of the company's temporary employees are 60 years or older.

"Nurturing" present employees in order to cut down on turnover is another way of "revolutionizing" the workforce. (For Pepsico's Pizza Hut chain, this takes the form of providing more appealing uniforms, improving the working environment and management styles, and testing a tuition-aid plan.)

Diamond (1989) maintains that living through these policies—from Medicare to Medicaid—is a *process* by which one becomes a pauper. "On public aid, nursing home life is the life of a pauper" is the way Diamond stated this argument. The process, if it begins with a private pay arrangement for care (e.g., the nursing home care being paid for through private funding), can start with a relatively high quality of care and environment, deteriorating as one "moves" into Medicare-paid care. Further deterioration of care and environment can occur as one moves from Medicare to Medicaid. Pauperism is not a dignified state, but is one that many elderly must settle for. For many nursing home residents, pauperism is accompanied by the loss of dignity incurred through institutionalism. Nursing homes, on average, are generally understaffed and underfunded, making adequate personal attention a rare commodity. To reside in a nursing home often means suffering personal indignities.

Although we hold to the view that people, not the government, are responsible for their own destinies, government's involvement in our lives has been part of the American tradition, although a fairly weak part. But welfare capitalism and industrial paternalism on the part of private industry became popular in the late 1800s as a response to worker militancy.

As capitalists began giving concessions in the form of workmen's compensation and other worker-betterment programs, they began at the same time to scale down programs when workers suspected them of covering up basic unmet needs. A shift of society's social needs onto the government's shoulders took place before World War II, but the government proved itself relatively ineffective, and certainly inefficient, in performing this function well. Therefore, industrial capitalism became prominent again in the 1960s and government took a back seat once more, a position it maintains today and one that is relatively weak compared to the position of governments in other countries such as Sweden, West Germany, and Great Britain.

The need for welfare capitalism is indicated not only by the number of caregivers in the workforce, but by the amount of effort they are making to give care and the effects upon their work of those caregiving responsibilities. Jobs must become more attractive through enhanced benefits in order to attract the best workers and to cope with a shrinking labor supply. A shrinking labor supply sets the stage for competition among firms in providing for workers' social needs.

Family concerns increasingly became workplace concerns as more two-career couples appeared in the workforce and as the number of single parents, both men and women, increased. Employers must become partners in addressing employee caregiving responsibilities. These workplace concerns include absenteeism and turnover, and deteriorating job performance and productivity. Enhancing worker productivity is an issue to which companies must respond. Lagging productivity is not only a concern to individual firms but to the entire nation as well, as we strive to remain competitive in the world market. Productivity deduces from the efforts of human capital, so any efforts to enhance human capital have the potential for enhancing productivity.

Turnover, absenteeism, and lower productivity are costly to a company. Ninety-three percent of the annual salary for a position typically is spent recruiting and training a new worker (Sandroff 1989); for every three dollars spent on employee assistance, four are saved because of reduced absenteeism, turnover, and productivity. But biases against flexible schedules and leave allowances, for example, which would retain valuable workers, notably women, still exist. Studies show, however, that women who take childbirth leave from companies with liberal leave policies are more likely to return to work than those who take leave from companies without such policies. Leave-taking by a woman, too, often signals the employer that she is less than serious about her job.

The meanings that workers assign to working and to their jobs have implications for productivity as well. Work holds both intrinsic and extrinsic meanings for workers. Intrinsic meaning is derived from the mere personal satisfaction of doing the work and receiving self-fulfillment through it. Extrinsic satisfaction is found in the economic rewards one receives from working. Both extrinsic and intrinsic meanings become enhanced by offering incentives to work—compensation, benefits, pleasant working environments, and such. When one of these incentives is missing, work can have less meaning and can incur decreasing satisfaction. The incentive to increase productivity may also lag as a result.

Another rationale for industry, both private and public, to be involved in solving the home-work dilemma has to do with the increasing impoverishment of children and young adults. A trend with important implications for quality of life is that much less of our GNP per capita is being spent on children than on the elderly; young adults are experiencing a decline in net wealth. Inflationary forces have caused much of this decline; one way to somewhat offset it is for employers, with the aid of government and other sources, to play a more active role in family assistance.

Businesses need to pay heed to the social needs of workers simply because it is good business to do so. When William Popejoy elected not to eliminate a company-sponsored day care center as his company was bailing out the American Savings and Loan Association of California, he believed it was good business practice to do so; employees with peace of mind are more productive workers (Fierman 1988). Such a measure was felt to have been cost-effective because it improved the bottom line of the company.

Attending to the family-business connection is good business, so say Rodgers and Rodgers (1989). Yet relatively few companies openly acknowledge the mismatch between the "rules of the game" (rules by which modern-day families with two wage earners abide) and the needs of the players (to accommodate these rules to the rules followed at work). A mismatch exists between work rules—a rigid 40-hour work week, equaling number of hours of work with productivity—and the daily contingencies arising at home—dependent care arrangements and maintenance, for example.

Matching up these two worlds in an accommodating and flexible atmosphere makes good sense. First of all, with the changing demographics (a smaller age cohort entering the labor market), there are higher costs to businesses associated with discouraging entry into the labor force, and more talented people who are trying to do a good job both at home and at work. Second, for career women who are parents, meeting barriers to advancement at work often causes them to change jobs, and women who would seek a career in the first place are discouraged by the lack of flexibility that would allow them to act responsibly both toward job and family. Men and women respond to inflexibility in the workplace by not accepting promotions, by extensive travel, overtime, or relocation. Many believe that if it were not for inflexibility, they could go further in their careers. But men are beginning to feel the results of this mismatch, too. Their reports of certain family-related problems (in two studies at DuPont) nearly doubled from 1985 to 1988.

Third, inflexibility is shown to have an adverse effect on productivity. Those who perceive their supervisors as unsupportive of family issues (in the Rodgers and Rodgers study), report high levels of stress, greater absenteeism, and lower job satisfaction than those who see their supervisors as supportive.

Finally, our children are suffering in many ways because of the lack of flexibility to parents on the part of businesses. SAT scores are declining, childhood poverty is increasing, and literacy and suicide rates among the young are on the rise. Working parents need to be able to become more involved in their childrens' school by attending teacher-parent conferences and important school events, anything that will enhance the parent-school connection. According to the studies of Rodgers and Rodgers, one-third of one-half of parents maintain that they lack the workplace flexibility that would allow them to attend these school events.

Rodgers and Rodgers point to three broad areas that need businesses' attention: dependent care assistance, greater flexibility in the organization, hours, and location of work, and validation of family issues as a business concern. They also note that the various costs of these areas to employers and employees are not inconsiderable. Dependent care program development may involve purchasing benefits and programs from outside the business, assumptions about work must be reexamined if flexibility is to be achieved, and it takes time for the corporate commitment to family to work its way "down the line" where the workforce will feel its effects. But the inference is that the effects far outweigh the costs.

NOTES

1. Arguments against businesses being social welfare providers speak to the fact that the real business of business is business; that shareholders' dollars should not be used for social welfare of employees and that employers should not be regarded as social safety

nets (Kamerman and Kahn 1987: 21). But the converse argument is that it should be private industry's response to the conflict between work and family rather than the response of government because government programs tend to be run inefficiently and are thus ineffective. At a 1980 White House Conference on Families, 92 percent of the delegates recommended that business-initiated, family-oriented personnel policies be implemented.

2. In 1990, private-pay patients in Colorado Springs nursing homes are paying from $22,000 to $28,000 a year for care.

3. A "new" school of thought on how to bring inflation under control holds that it can be done by stimulating supply through increased productivity, among other things.

4. Macarov (1982: 105) suggests that through the use of automated office equipment, managers and professionals could increase their productivity 15 percent within five years. As to a specific setting, McDonald's is trying out a grill that cooks hamburgers on both sides at once.

5. That the meanings people attach to work lie along a continuum is also suggested by the results of surveys I conducted in my Sociology of Work classes at Regis College. In most cases, students and those they have surveyed work for the salary and benefits as well as for self-enrichment and the challenge it gives.

6. This view of meanings, incentives, and productivity undoubtedly is a gross oversimplification. For instance, efforts to humanize work, to make it more satisfying, and to increase productivity at the same time may work at cross purposes. For a more elaborate discussion of these concerns, see Macarov (1982), chapter 6.

7. Dychtwald and Flower's book, *Age Wave* (1989) is an excellent account of this unbalance between the economic power of the elderly and the young.

8. Indicating the need to respond to a labor shortage is the "message" inferred in a cartoon in the February, 1990 issue of the AARP *Bulletin*. It depicts a crouching person with a butterfly net just inside the door next to a window on which there is a sign reading "Help Wanted. See Manager."

3

Policies and Programs

This chapter is devoted to discussing the various employee assistance plans adopted and available that accommodate the dependent care needs of workers. The prevalence (or lack) of these benefits in public and private sector firms is noted. The rationale for these plans is discussed, along with descriptions of plans in specific firms. Finally, problems of generating and implementing the various benefits are acknowledged and recommendations are given.

An employee benefits plan is defined as any provision for income maintenance, released time, vacation time, or personal time, sponsored or initiated unilaterally or jointly by employers and employees, whose basis is the employment relationship not under direct government sponsorship (Kamerman and Kahn 1987: 37).

Several forms of employee assistance plans are recognized: a flexible spending account/cafeteria plan; the provision of information through handbooks, manuals, brochures, seminars, and caregiver fairs; parental and disability leave; child care assistance in an off- or on-site facility; consortia and coalitions comprised of several firms; flextime work scheduling; a voucher system; and tax credits.[1]

The issue of providing assistance to workers who have dependent care responsibilities is vital in the 1990s. Interest in and attention to this issue are lively and recent (see the several articles cited in *The Wall Street Journal*, and note not only the length of this book's reference list but the dates on most of the citations), and continue to capture the attention of both private and public industries, unions, advocate groups, state and federal legislatures, the public, and the media.

Public response to the issue is noted in a recent survey of voter opinion conducted by State Senator Ray Powers (CO). On the issue of day care for children, 67 percent of those surveyed supported tax credits for parents, and 75 percent supported tax incentives for businesses that want to set up day care centers for employees without using state or federal subsidies. States' involvement in the dependent care issue is noted in *The Wall Street Journal* (January 4, 1989), stating that, to that date, 22 states plus the District of Columbia offered benefits to cover some dependent care costs. Those benefits take the form of personal income tax credits as a percentage of the federal tax credit (the median allowed is 25 percent), deductions or credits based on expenses, and, to employers, a 30 percent credit of up to $30,000 for the cost of establishing a child care program or facility for employees plus a 50 percent credit of up to $600 a year per employee for costs of the plan's operation.

Industries' response to the issue is commented on by Fierman (1988), Martin and Hartley (1975), Stonebaker (1984), and others. In a survey conducted by Louis Harris and Associates, as of 1985, 20 percent of the surveyed companies offered a flexible spending account/cafeteria plan to employees; 46 percent of management personnel, however, expected their companies to introduce this plan in the following two years. By the end of 1982, although only 6 percent of the firms responding to another survey claimed to be offering this plan, one-quarter expected to do so in the near future. It is estimated by Fierman (1988) that approximately 1,500 companies nationwide provide flexible spending accounts. Banking and insurance organizations are better represented in the flexible provision than are manufacturing firms. Mellor (1986) maintains that by May, 1985, 12 percent of all full-time workers were on flextime work schedules. Those most likely to be in this arrangement were in executive, administrative, managerial, and sales occupations. Twenty-nine percent of managers in U.S. companies polled in one survey now have some form of flextime.

The Conference Board late in 1985 discovered that 2,500 companies are providing some form of child care assistance, and this number seems to be increasing. Of this number, 400 are located at hospitals, 150 at corporations, and 30 at public agencies; 150 offer a cafeteria plan, 75 an after-school child care plan, 25 offer vouchers, and 20 have a sick child

care initiative. One thousand provide corporate contributions to local child care programs. The Board predicts that corporate financial contributions will grow in popularity followed by contributions to community-based care. The trend is for employees to "buy into" already existing dependent care plans at the workplace. This "buying in" reduces employer liability.

But a questionnaire survey by Levine (1984) reveals that, although 86 percent of human resource managers felt a need for child care policies, only 14 percent of their companies had or were currently sponsoring a day care program. (Fifty-one percent of the total respondents offered permanent part-time work and 50 percent offered flexible working hours.)[2]

Martin and Hartley (1975) report that the concept and implementation of rearranged work schedules (flextime scheduling) was discovered among members of the American Society of Personnel Administration Managers and Administrators. The "discovery" was made in companies ranging in size from 9 employees to those with 36,800 workers, to include those in insurance, finance, retail trade, manufacturing, medical services, and libraries. (The response rate from the survey was 42 percent; 33 percent of the respondents provided usable data.) Types of rearranged work scheduling included staggered hours that were employer-assigned, unspecified staggered hours, unspecified flexible hours, the four-day and three-day work week, permanent part-time, and a task system arrangement whereby work hours are not counted but completion of the task is. In 1980, 2.7 percent of the full-time adult labor force worked on a compressed (flextime) work schedule (up from 1.7 percent in 1973).

Flextime was mandated for federal agencies in 1978 with the passing of the Federal Employees Flexible and Compressed Work Schedules Act. The act established a three-year experiment in flexible hours. By 1980, 7.16 million workers (12 percent of all full-time workers excluding self-employed and farm workers) were working flexible schedules. Another 2.7 million part-time workers reported that they had the option to depart from fixed work schedules (Pleck 1986). One in five workers in federal public administration jobs reported they were on a flexible schedule. Flexible work schedules were most prominent in sales, managerial, and administrative jobs, and among professionals, technical, and transport equipment workers.

The Center for the Study of Aging at the University of Bridgeport, Connecticut, was awarded a grant from the U.S. Administration of Aging during 1986–1987. The Center used the funds to determine the extent of elder caregiving responsibilities and attendant problems among employees of Pitney Bowes, People's Bank, and Remington Products Corporations, firms that varied in size from 1,000 to 40,000 employees (Pitney Bowes has an international workforce). At the time, over 25 percent of the respondents among the three firms claimed to be involved in caregiving. The responsibilities most frequently managed by employees were the provision of transportation and meals, followed by the arranging of appointments.

Growth in the number of private sector child day care programs was noted by Burud et al. (1983). As of spring 1982, 415 private sector programs were operating, representing an increase of 296 percent from 1978. Gold (1989) states that the separation of work and home is "eroding" with more and more businesses embracing the idea of child care centers in office buildings. He notes that corporations, colleges, real estate developers, politicians, and city planners are endorsing centers. On-site care centers emerged in the 1960s and are the "wave of the future," claims the head of a counseling firm in Pasadena, California. Increasingly developers are including day care centers in their office building plans. In Chicago an ordinance recently was proposed requiring office developers to subsidize day care centers. Cities such as Los Angeles are considering offering various incentives to builders, and in Montgomery County, Maryland, the planning board in February, 1989, approved a shopping mall/office complex with the condition that the developer help build and operate a care center.

Not only has there been a growth in the number of dependent care assistance plans, but expenditures on these plans as a proportion of payroll have been on the increase. In 1959, 24.4 percent of a firm's payroll was represented by employee benefit payments; in 1969 it was 31 percent; in 1979, 41.2 percent. Employee benefit payments per year per worker were $1,200 in 1959; in 1979 they were over $6,000. This growth is a response, to an extent at least, to changing demographics.

A comprehensive study of the scope and outcomes of private sector industry child day care programs was undertaken from 1981 to 1983 by the Child Care Information Service of Pasadena, California. The Service found that of the company-sponsored programs, the most prevalent child care program provider was business and industry; 195 of these programs were in hospitals, 17 in public agencies, and 5 under union sponsorship. A wide variety of services existed within these employment contexts, such as information and referral services, support from community programs, on- and near-site child day care (the most prevalent), voucher reimbursement plans, and parent education programs. Companies that sponsor some kind of child care services ranged in size from less than one hundred to more than five thousand employees. Those most likely to have a program had a preponderance (nearly three-quarters) of women in their employment; banks and insurance companies are two examples.

A study was sponsored by the National Association of Area Agencies on Aging (of which there are 670 nationwide) and funded through grant money awarded by the Administration on Aging to discover the responsibilities, profiles, and implications of caregiving of working caregivers.[3] The benefit getting the highest number of votes in terms of preference for future benefits to aid working caregivers was a cafeteria benefit, followed closely by respite care benefits. Reduced working hours and an adult day care program received the next highest number of votes followed by job-sharing and flextime. From this study came the suggestion that Area Agencies on Aging can cooperate to plan benefits for workers to support work as well as to increase productivity. One suggestion was for a cooperative effort to discover the prevalence and dimensions of caregivers and caregiving, the creation of greater awareness of those needs, and the sponsorship of workshops to inform working caregivers of community resources. Establishing training sessions for personnel counselors was also suggested from the study.

COALITIONS AND CONSORTIA

The formation of coalitions and consortia is one means by which work organizations can accommodate workers' dependent caregiving needs. Joining a consortium of caregivers in the company's area is another method of corporate support. One coalition, in the Metropolitan Chicago area, deals in marketing seminars and referral services to companies. Such services as technical assistance to member agencies is another option (Friedman 1986).

A public-private consortium of 17 in San Francisco was formed under the rubric of the California Child Care Initiative. Some of the goals are to build on an existing state resource to increase the supply of child care providers by using resource and referral agencies, to train new providers, and to underwrite efforts of community providers and referral agencies. Nearly 1,100 new child care spaces were created in the state under this initiative. They are located in Contra Costa County, San Francisco, Sacramento, Los Angeles, Long Beach, and Bakersfield.

A dependent care assistance arrangement in the form of a consortium including Dayton-Hudson, Pillsbury, and Northern States Power Company, all of Minneapolis, was formed. The program eventually serviced mainly community people (but was phased out because of changed residential patterns and the aging of children of employees).[4] A consortium of seven New York City companies (e.g., Time, Inc. and Colgate-Palmolive) has been formed to provide home assistance to workers who have a sick child or ill babysitter (*Wall Street Journal* May 23, 1989).

State involvement in dependent caregiving needs and those of the disabled is widely recognized. For instance, in New Jersey, pregnancy is treated like any other condition that prevents an employee from working. Temporary Disability Insurance (TDI) covers leave for a maximum of 26 weeks. To be eligible, the employee must have worked at least 20 weeks and earned more than $76 a week during that year or must have earned a total of $4,300 for that year. The eligible employee can receive two-thirds of her average weekly wage. The package is paid for by both employer and employee, each paying .5 percent of an employee's earnings not to exceed $53.50 a week. Almost all employers that employ one or more persons and whose earnings are at least $1,000 a year must contribute to the state's TDI fund or have a private disability plan on board.

In-home emergency day care is another mode being tried by a few organizations. In New York City, Home Box Office, Colgate-Palmolive, National Westminster Bank U.S.A., Time, Inc., the Ernst and Young accounting firm, and Consolidated Edison Company plan to begin a year-long experiment to provide an in-home day care service to parents in emergencies. A spokesperson for the plan acknowledged that the arrangement will provide a backup system of child care assistance where there are no other alternatives, such as an available extended family, when the child of a working parent becomes ill and cannot go to school, when a parent is unexpectedly called away on business, or where the family's regular child care arrangement fails to materialize. When these events take place, it becomes a stressful situation for the employee and subsequently for the employer, said the spokesperson.

LEAVES OF ABSENCE

The most common leaves that companies grant are maternity/parental and disability leaves. Child care and parental leaves are becoming more common. Options regarding leave-taking are available with each type.

Extended leave policies are being adopted by more firms. Beginning January 1, 1990, AT&T allowed workers to take up to a year of unpaid leave every two years of employment; they retain seniority and are guaranteed jobs upon their return. During the first six months of leave, employees receive full medical and dental benefits. AT&T plans also to establish a $45 million seed-money fund to set up or expand eldercare facilities wherever its workers are located. Hallmark Cards, Inc. offers a flexible benefit plan covering such out-of-pocket medical expenses for dependents as eye glasses and hearing aids and some health-related travel costs. The plan is funded by a flexible spending account that lets employees set aside pretax earnings for eldercare.

A study made by Catalyst's Career and Family Center (1986b), in which 384 responses from larger corporations were studied, identified policies in place, how they operated, attitudes of employers toward leave-taking, and characteristics of corporations. Over one-half of the responding industries were engaged in manufacturing, construction, mining, or agriculture; over one-quarter were in financial or service businesses. Aspects of parental leave policies relevant to the study were: adoption benefits, anticipated and current leave to include pregnancy leave, benefits allowed according to tenure, and length of leave. Eligibility and limited part-time return and reinstatement policies, seniority and loss thereof, unpaid leave, and the effects on subsequent time off or leave-taking were addressed as well.[5]

Most of the respondents in this study claimed to offer *at least* partially paid disability leave (over 38 percent offered fully paid leave), with most companies (90.2 percent) continuing full benefits such as insurance to employees on leave. In a majority of cases (63 percent), five to eight weeks of leave was the average length of disability leave taken by women; only 4.7 percent took from one to four weeks. The length of leave was usually dependent upon the conditions of reinstatement. In the cases of both managerial and nonmanagerial women, the most frequently reported length of leave taken, both disability and unpaid, was three to eight weeks followed by from nine to 12 weeks. In only about 13 percent of the cases was some kind of job reinstatement not guaranteed; a few less offered the "same job" than offered a "comparable job." In just fewer than one-half of the cases, part-time employees were not offered the option of parental leave. Part-time employees in just over 28 percent of the firms were eligible for full parental leave benefits. Unpaid leaves to women and adoption benefits were most frequently offered in transportation, communication, and utilities industries.

Eligibility for leave-taking varies by company, but a study reported by Sheinberg (1988) noted that most employees of medium and large firms need at least six months of service to qualify for sickness or vacation benefits, and 84 percent of the firms have some minimum service requirement to qualify for a maternity leave. In another study, 50 percent of larger firms had no service requirement for a leave, whereas 20 percent had a service requirement of only three months.[6]

Length of leave varied as well. One study reported that 61 percent of the respondents offered a two- to three-month leave. In another study, less than 50 percent of the respondent companies offered a maximum leave of between four to six months, and in yet another, the average unpaid leave granted to women was three months or less. The typical leave offered in both small and large companies ranges from a minimal disability period of a few weeks to several months or even a year (in rare cases).

Reimbursement during an extended leave usually does not represent an employee's full salary, according to the Sheinberg study. Only 39 percent of the largest companies that responded to a survey offered full reimbursement for disabled employees during leave; 57 percent paid only a portion of salary.

Parental leave for fathers takes several different forms to include: (1) long-term paid leave at time of a child's birth, (2) short-term paid leave at time of a child's birth, (3) unpaid leave at time of a child's birth, (4) reduced work time allowing time to spend with young children, and (5) personal or child care days. The latter two are found infrequently in U.S. firms. In the case of long-term paid and unpaid leave at time of a child's birth, the Ford Foundation provides a paid child care leave of eight weeks and additional unpaid leave of 18 weeks. Leave must be taken within the first six months after the employee becomes a parent. Employees taking leave are assured of returning to a comparable job or the same job if possible. Benefits continue during paid leave-taking. In the case of unpaid leave, contributions to retirement and savings plans are exempted; all other benefits accrue during leave (Lamb 1986).

The use of leave-taking by men is not necessarily usual, however. A Catalyst (1986a) study discovered that over a third of the respondent corporations offered an unpaid parental leave with a job guarantee to men, but few men take advantage of this policy. Only 9 companies out of 384 reported men taking parental leave. If paternity leave is taken by men, it is usually under a vacation or personal leave arrangement. Some companies reported it "inappropriate" for men to take paternity leave. The study revealed, in fact, that over 62 percent of the corporate respondents considered "no leave time" as reasonable for men to take. Even in companies having unpaid leave policies for men, leave-taking was not necessarily sanctioned.

RETURNING TO WORK

Sheinberg (1988) remarks that facilitating the return to work after leave-taking is another dependent care matter to which companies are beginning to respond. A limited part-time work option is available in many companies for both management and nonmanagement personnel, according to Sheinberg. With this option, a manager can rearrange job responsibilities in order to be able to do the same amount of work in fewer hours and/or by delegating work. This option is more difficult for managers because of their oft-times indispensability. However, a nonmanagement employee will often find her part-time work to be in a different job from the one she left, sometimes causing her to forfeit accrued benefits and former salary level. Nonetheless, such an option often encourages employees to return to work sooner than planned, thus making it possible for a company to get back a valuable worker sooner.

In terms of preferences on return-to-work policies, the Catalyst (1986a) study revealed that many women preferred to ease back into work by way of part-time employment or on a flexible schedule. (Women apparently valued having the opportunity to make a gradual re-entry.) Sixty percent of the respondents in this study reported that these types of return-to-work arrangements were offered to both managers and nonmanagers, although such an arrangement is easier to handle by nonmanagerial employees.

The handling of work left by both managerial and nonmanagerial leave-takers was addressed in a high proportion of respondents in the Catalyst (1986a) study by rerouting the work to others in the department. In a high percentage of the cases, the mode of handling work of managerial leave-takers was considered satisfactory. The method of handling the work of nonmanagerial leave-takers was to hire a temporary from outside the firm, followed by rerouting work to others in the department and the use of temporary replacement from inside the firm.[7]

RELUCTANCE TO LEAVE POLICIES

The reasons given to the Catalyst (1986b) "reporters" for companies' reluctance to expand parental leave options were productivity and turnover concerns and legal or equity issues. Productivity of a position is dependent upon continuity of work, among other things, so the handling of leave-takers' work ad hoc rather than on a consistent and in-advance basis can be a problem. But turnover is often the result of policies that restrict too severely the length of leave, causing leave-takers to return to work before they are physically and/or emotionally ready, and, therefore, discouraging the continuance of work. And the cost of turnover is high; for any position, it can cost up to 93 percent of a first-year salary and can far outweigh the costs of a generous leave policy.

Depending upon how employees feel about the "legitimacy" and validity of maternity leave, the equity of leave policies can be problematic as well. In certain corporate cultures, employees who are not parents may resent leave options for parents. In such cases, a general personal leave-of-absence policy that includes all types of leaves, including parental, may be appropriate and may skirt the problem of seeming to offer leaves of different length to women and men.

CASE STUDIES: LEAVES

General Foods Corporation of White Plains, New York, with 35,000 workers throughout the country, provides unpaid child care leave with job assurance, up to 6 weeks of leave following the birth of a baby or adoption. This 6 weeks may be taken in addition to maternity leave. All insurance coverage is continued during leave if the employee continues to make contributions to the insurance program. Personal leave time of up to 12 months is allowed, but there are no return-to-work rights with this much leave. Flexible time scheduling and part-time and job-sharing are also part of the firm's benefits and may be arranged for up to one year after birth or adoption.

Fel-Pro, Inc., of Skokie, Illinois, allows personal and maternity leave. The firm also offers counseling and referral services as well as providing a day care center for two- to five-year-olds.

At Merck and Company, Inc. in Rahway, New Jersey, maternity and child care leaves without pay are allowed; men may also take advantage of child care leave. With these two programs, up to 6 months leave assures job reinstatement; from 6 to 18 months, there is no job guarantee and after 18 months of leave, employment is terminated. Personal leaves of absence to care for a sick child are allowed as well with the continuance of insurance assured.

The Bank Street College of Education, New York City, in 1980 began offering 3 months of paid leave coverage to both parents. At first, it was offered only to the professional staff but was extended to service employees in 1986.

SEMINARS, FAIRS, INFORMATION SERVICES,
VOUCHER AND TAX-ADVANTAGED PROGRAMS

Probably the easiest way to deliver service to caregiving employees is through an information package about policy. Winfield (1987) suggests posting notices in the workplace, holding lunchtime seminars, fairs, and support group meetings at work, the distribution of handbooks and advertising company library resources as some of the ways to communicate company dependent care policies. Critical to the effectiveness of a support group plan is having leaders knowledgeable about community resources that can be accessed.

Pitney Bowes maintains a Child Care Resource and Referral Service, a program providing information on types of child care available, child care providers with openings, and child care regulations. A provider is not selected by Pitney Bowes but is chosen by the employee through the referral process.

The Information and Referral Service located in the Metropolitan Washington, D.C., area provides a child care network funded by corporate and other contributions. The service gives the phone numbers of service providers (but no recommendations). The network service is now doing recruiting and training of new child care providers. This service receives about 31,000 calls each year. Pathfinders, a Scarsdale, New York, case management and counseling service, was hired by Con Edison, Ciba-Geigy, and Mobil to provide information seminars. It is suggested that such on-site services, offered through a firm's medical, legal, or personnel department, reduce employee's search time for needed dependent care services. The Metropolitan Chicago Coalition on Aging, through its Aging in the Workplace Project, assists member agencies in the marketing of seminars and referral services.

Lunch or after-hours seminars and caregiver fairs, usually conducted on-site, are viable ways to disseminate information on caregiving. These sessions often are staffed by outside resources; in this case, companies contract for services to be rendered. Material forthcoming from these sessions can be distributed through a company's personnel and/or medical office.

Several information packets to be dispensed at these sessions and to a general employee pool are now available. The Administration on Aging has a resource guidebook, "Where to Turn for Help for Older Persons." Another, "Caregivers in the Workplace," is a planning guide and training manual to help human resource personnel organize aid to caregivers of the elderly. The guide has four components: a survey to assess prevalence and needs of caregiving and caregivers; advice on organizing noon-hour fairs where community service organizations dispense information and field questions; 10 one-hour training programs that can be offered, which address needs of caregiving employees; and a resource guide for counselors in such "offices" as employee assistance.

The American Association of Retired Persons (AARP) has taken the initiative in raising employer awareness of working caregivers' problems through a kit generated by the Women's Initiative of Caregivers in the Workplace. The "rationale" is to help workers maintain their productivity levels, to reduce their work-family stress, and to provide them with information and resources to deal with caregiving responsibilities. The four components of the kit include a survey that can be administered to determine the prevalence of caregivers in a firm and to assess their caregiver needs, a guideline for implementing a session during which community service organizations answer questions and distribute literature, a care management guide providing counselors with information needed to help employees find services, and a 10-hour educational module package including resource materials and instructions for trainers.[8]

A booklet prepared for PepsiCo of Bridgeport, Connecticut, by the University of Bridgeport's Center for the Study of Aging describes physical aging, psychological and emotional development in later life, enhancement of later life, physical and mental conditions of aging, and financial, health, and community resources available to the elderly. Financial resources described include Social Security, Medicare, supplemental security income, and privately arranged financial coverage. Community resources described include information and referral services, various types of housing (e.g., life care communities), nutrition and transportation programs, counseling, and home health and homemaker services.

PepsiCo itself has developed a hotline for eldercare assistance and tax-advantaged plans for eldercare. Reserve accounts for health and day care are available to those who qualify. Under these plans, called Benefits Plus, employees may set aside money from their earnings, before taxes, to pay for medical and dependent care expenses of employees, their spouse and children, and elder dependents. A reserve of five thousand dollars may cover out-of-pocket expenses including medical, dental, vision, hearing, home health care, and nursing homes. The same amount may be reserved to pay for day care for dependent elders such as adult day care and in-home supervised eldercare. Money reserved for the particular year must be used or forfeited, and is committed during the annual Benefits Plus enrollment program in the fall.

Eldercare referral services are gaining popularity with the realization that so many employees are faced with such responsibilities. Work/Family Elder Directions, Inc., a firm in Watertown, Massachusetts, offers elder-care consultation and referral services for a growing number of clients including IBM, Xerox, McDonald's, and Merrill Lynch. Such services link employees with a range of services such as nursing homes, hospices, nutritionists, and elderly recreational facilities.

A series of six brown-bag, lunchtime seminars on elderly caregiving was recently sponsored by a retirement residential facility and held at a Colorado Springs, Colorado, high-tech firm. The series addressed the legal considerations of elder caregiving such as financial planning devices, guardianship, and conservatorship; senior housing options and community-based resources were addressed. One session spoke to the processes of aging; another to the issues arising in caregiving itself (e.g., emotional, physical). One session informed attendees of health matters of the aging; another described such programs as Medicare, Medicaid, and long-term care insurance. AARP supported this seminar series by providing packets of information, as did the Pikes Peak Area Agency on Aging.

Ingersoll-Dayton et al. (1990) describe an eldercare program generated in four metropolitan Portland, Oregon, firms: a manufacturing company, bank, insurance agency, and public agency. The first phase of the program was to survey 33 companies' employees about their eldercare responsibilities. Of the 9,573 respondents, 23 percent provided care to elders. The average age of participants was 45. Sixty-three percent of these were sole or main caregivers, 25 percent lived with their dependents, and 78 percent lived within 25 miles of them. Just over 14 percent of the participants were men.

The second phase of the program was to provide eldercare services of various types to employees at four worksites. One of the services was a seven-week educational seminar series followed by participants choosing among three service options, each running for eight weeks. One of these service options included care planning (the case management approach), a support group of peers facilitated by two professionals, and a one-on-one peer support arrangement pairing employees in a similar situation. The seminar series was conducted during the lunch hour and between afternoon shifts (in the manufacturing firm). Topics covered were normal physical aging, common emotional problems, community services, financial, legal, Medicare, and Medicaid concerns, and long-term insurance. Residential options, caregiver wellness, and juggling work and family were other topics. The most requested assistance was on the topics of physical changes, emotional problems, Medicare, Medicaid, and long-term care.

If a participant chose the care planning option, the caregiving situation was assessed, possible resources were suggested, and a need assessment of the elderly dependent was made. In the support group, participants met with co-employees and two professionals to discuss various topics pertaining to caregiving situations.

The seminar series was rated by participants as "very helpful." Because of the seminars, knowledge of available services increased among participants, and many of them tried new approaches in communicating to their elders. Knowledge of resources and of ways to care for the elderly were reported enhanced by the care planning option participants.

The National Council on Aging, Washington, D.C., a private, nonprofit organization concerned with the quality of life of elders, offers a bulletin entitled "Caregiving Tips: How to Find and Use Community Services." The programs, agencies, and resources listed in this bulletin are an area agency on aging, the council or office on aging, the Social Security district office, the department of social services, a senior center, an adult care program, home care agencies, family service agencies, private geriatric counselors or care managers, geriatric physicians and nurses, churches, and community civic and service groups. Readers are advised to locate these resources in their telephone books. The bulletin suggests ways to seek and use resources such as zeroing in on the real need, exploring eligibility requirements, checking out procedures, and having documents and records handy.

Boris Gertz, clinical consultant and staff development specialist in Denver, Colorado, offers programs for professional and personal development such as management and organization development, clinical consultation and training, and support for caregivers in an organization. There is a module on support for and the identification of caregivers in the workplace, how caregiving affects work and productivity, types of consultation, and training and education services at work to assist employees with caregiving.

Financial support to a firm's dependent caregivers can take the form of vouchers to be used by employees at local child care centers, for the expenses of day care at home or for a caregiver who comes to the parent's home. Corporations can also reserve slots in local care centers and pay for them as they are filled.

Polaroid Corporation of Cambridge, Massachusetts, provides a voucher service to its employees needing dependent care assistance. The company pays a subsidy to cover a percentage of the day care bill, the amount determined by the employee's income. Approximately 100 employees a year use this system. Polaroid uses several area providers for its voucher program, paying 80 percent of an employee's child care bill where family income is minimal.

Another information-dissemination mode under trial is the teleconference. At a Colorado Springs high-tech firm, 24 individuals attended a national teleconference on September 22, 1989, in the company's conference center. The following themes were addressed: parallels and complements of eldercare and child care, long-distance caregiving, and coordinating resources and funding of the private sector with networks, programs, services, and agencies from the public sector. Centralized clearinghouses for caregiving referrals and information, and a focused communications network were other dominant themes. During this conference, discussions included the need for tighter coordination with educational agencies and systems regarding eldercare; the need for placement/services for the developmentally disabled; deficiencies such as the lack of coordination of resources and efforts among the public and private sectors; the confusion caused by a multiplicity of agencies, programs, and services due to the many levels within agencies; and the lack of consistent process or standards within and among agencies. Workshops with employees and staff to develop ideas for handling eldercare, care fairs, and meetings with state government personnel by corporate officials were suggested as ways to address employees' needs for eldercare assistance. At this teleconference, beamed to 12 cities and sponsored by the National Conference on the Aging, participants heard the suggestion that as society continues to age, workers who care for an aging parent will need increasing support in the workplace. Less than 15 percent of all employers now offer flexible hours that permit employees to care for an older person, a fact that causes an estimated 12 percent of workers to leave their jobs.

ON- AND NEAR-SITE CARE CENTERS

Government-funded corporate day care programs proliferated in the 1960s but dwindled in the 1970s when funds began to dry up. Although on-site care centers are now rare, several companies have found them to be a viable and attractive alternative to other forms of employee assistance. Their attractiveness lies in their convenience and almost-immediate accessibility to employees. The Bureau of National Affairs reports that on-site care centers are quite appropriate at hospitals, for example. Boston City Hospital established such a center in 1982 through the efforts of the Service Employees International Union, Local 285, a union of clerks, technicians, nurses, and licensed practical nurses comprising a group of about 2,000 persons. Sixteen slots are provided, eleven of them subsidized by the city.

A near-site center, also in Boston, was established by Hill Holliday Connors Cosmopulos, Inc., where there are 350 workers. This advertising and public relations firm opened its center in 1985 in a church three blocks away. (The impetus for establishing the center was the desire not to lose two vice presidents who were pregnant.)

PAC International in North Carolina operates a child care center. Well staffed with highly qualified and highly paid employees, the center is open until midnight.

The Allendale Insurance Company of Rhode Island and Union Mutual Life of Portland, Maine, have dependent care arrangements with a large child care chain in their respective regions (Kamerman and Kahn 1987). Under this arrangement, employees receive a discount on fees in exchange for assurance of a guaranteed minimum enrollment.

Union Planters National Bank of Memphis, Tennessee, has a discounted day care arrangement that amounts to receiving a percentage discount for day care services provided by a specific facility. Employees receive a discounted child care rate, and the day care provider receives a larger customer base from Union Planters referrals. According to Janet Haflich, compensation analyst for Union Planters, day care providers simply contact the bank to work out the details of what service or product will be provided, how the employee may receive the service or product, and other arrangements.

Stride Rite Shoes of Roxbury, Massachusetts, opened a children's center in May of 1971. A second center was opened in 1983 in Cambridge, where the company had moved its corporate headquarters. The centers provide care for both employees' and community children. When the centers opened, the concept of work-sponsored child care was relatively new. The nonprofit, incorporated centers are guided by a board of directors that includes two company and four community representatives, three parents, and each center's director.

In the last 10 years, corporate and noncorporate attention has been paid to Stride Rite's centers, with the company assisting in the development of over 50 such centers around the country. Periodic seminars have been held to inform executives interested in exploring the work-based child center idea. The centers have a close relationship with many community public and private social service agencies, making it possible for the center staff to give referrals to employees with regard to other social and medical needs.

The cost of this program is approximately $6,000 a year per child, a cost shared by the corporation, parents of children in the centers, and by the Massachusetts Department of Social Services. Additionally, the adjunct food program is partially funded by the U.S. Department of Agriculture's Bureau of Nutrition. Parent fees are based on income and amount to about 14 percent of gross pay. Subsidies from the Department of Social Services are available to low-income community families; the balance of the cost not picked up by the department is paid by the corporation.

A day care facility for sick children of working parents is provided in the Minneapolis area. Called Chicken Soup, the center opened in 1985. Children are brought to the center, examined by a nurse, and assigned to a room if necessary.

Recognizing that quality child care plays an important part in the lives of working parents, Excel-Nyloncraft of Mishawaka, Indiana, a company specializing in thermo-plastics injection molding and window systems and employing about five hundred persons in a union shop, set up an on-site "learning center" in 1981. A loss of productivity resulting from high turnover coupled with high training costs of new employees and excessive absenteeism spurred the firm's officers to do something about child care. Every job in the plant was turned over three times in 1978 and training costs were running as high as $2,000 per employee. It was discovered that child care concerns were at the root of these problems. Footwork to establish the center included researching corporate child care through articles, visits, and discussion with attorneys, accountants, and the state licensing department, assessing employee needs, and hiring a child care consultant.

The company chose an on-site rather than off-site facility to eliminate employee complaints about not wanting to use a subsidized outside child care facility, and the company also wanted to be able to control and monitor the center's activities and operation. But there was a particular problem that made establishing an on-site center difficult. State regulations for child care centers, such as not allowing the facility to be cleaned while children are on the premises, applied to centers open the usual 8-hour day, but three of the company's plants were open 24 hours a day. Many of the younger women employees without seniority worked the night shifts in these plants. This meant that a care center would have to be open at night as well to accommodate these workers with children. The "battle" was with the public Welfare Department, the licensing body for day care centers in Indiana. Management finally took its cause to the governor of the state, Otis Bowen.

Persistence paid off and the Nyloncraft Learning Center was opened as a subsidiary of Nyloncraft. Originally the facility, located next to the plant, was a leased unit needing complete renovation prior to occupancy. The unit included a 3,400-square-foot space with a 4,500-square-foot playground area; an open classroom concept was implemented. Fully equipped kitchen and laundry facilities were part of the center. Start-up costs included $100,000 for renovation and $50,000 for equipment, supplies, and such. Since its opening, the center has moved onto the plant site itself; renovation of this new unit cost $150,000. It includes 4,600 square feet of space with a 5,000-square-foot playground. The open classroom concept was retained as were the kitchen and laundry facilities. The new center is licensed to care for 120 children.

A new plant was built in 1983 in Mishawaka and it incorporates the 6,000-square-foot learning center down the hall from the general manager's office. Preschoolers are enrolled there and after-school care is offered as well. Half of the $63 per week tuition is subsidized and free care provided for workers putting in overtime. A cooperative service program with the local Montessori school, kindergarten and extended care, a summer day camp, transportation, services for disabled children, and enrichment trips are part of the center's activities and facility. It is staffed by licensed teachers, paraprofessional aides, and there is access to a clinical psychologist as a consultant. In-service training programs and a staff-to-child ratio of 1:8 are also provided. The center is open to the community.

In May, 1988, Nyloncraft was chosen by the Congressional Caucus for Women's Issues to receive a pioneer award in recognition for its initiating and developing "one of the most innovative employer-sponsored child care programs in the United States" (*Congressional Record*, May 5, 1988). The president of Nyloncraft, Jim Wylie, was cited as having recognized that child care is a business issue, for having made a commitment to helping families, having an "eye to the future," and having initiated the first 24-hour, on-site day care facility in the state of Indiana, a facility that is helping with the "care and development of our most precious and most important resource—our children."

Benefits to parents and children of the center are a child care tax credit for those filing the long IRS form, reduced anxiety over child care among employees, the close proximity to the workplace, educationally oriented programs for all ages, a "caring" atmosphere, and health screenings and nutritional meals. Benefits to the company are tax credits and deductions, a reduction in turnover and absenteeism, an increase in employee morale and retention, and positive public relations. To society as a whole, the benefits are seen as the provision of quality service to the community, the use of community resources, the provision of employment opportunities, and the cost of effectiveness of the programs.

In the fall of 1988, Patricia and Henley Zigler's School of the 21st Century was conceived under the notion of "day care for the masses," according to Fierman (1987). Funded by nearly $300,000 from local foundations and $50,000 from the Missouri Department of Education to renovate schools, the project has both a before- and after-school program and day care for three- and four-year-olds. Proceeds go into a scholarship fund for needy children.

A coalition of 33 public and private concerns, which includes the American Express Foundation and the City of Santa Monica, California, and is organized by the Bank of America as the California Child Care Initiative, has established 1,200 licensed day care homes to serve over 6,000 children. DuPont aided a number of community organizations to establish and expand existing child care centers in Delaware. Establishing and expanding can be done by donating space, land and renovation costs, or providing an initial subsidy until the centers are self-supporting (Rodgers and Rodgers 1989).

In Texas, the Houston Committee for Private Sector Initiatives, in 1982 started an after-school program for children of working parents. The program is offered in schools, churches, service organizations, and the YMCA, and receives corporate funding. A similar service operates in Denver, called Family Communication, Inc. It offers a device called the home companion, which enables children to notify their parents when they are home safely from school, and can notify the authorities of any medical, fire, or police emergencies. The device is connected to the home phone. If the child fails to press the device upon arrival from school or some predetermined time, a response center is alerted and calls the home. If there is no answer, a contact person or parent is called. The response center has data on children, their parents, and possible medical problems that may arise.

A partnership providing before- and after-school programs has been established between the American Bankers Insurance Group and the Dade County, Florida, school district. The insurance company erected a building in which there are kindergarten and first- and second-grade classrooms (Rodgers and Rodgers 1989).

FLEXTIME

The concept of flextime, or rearranged work scheduling, is attributed to Christel Kaemmerer, who conceived the idea in 1967 to relieve West Germany's labor shortage by bringing mothers into the workplace. Flextime has now become a common "response" to employees who must integrate their lives as parents with their lives as employees (Odiorne 1987). It is defined as a work schedule that offers, within certain boundaries, the opportunity to start and finish work at one's own time-discretion. Types of flextime include the compressed work week with three or four working days, the shortened day, working during various time-spans during the day, and part-time work either temporary or permanent. Job-sharing can be worked into a permanent part-time position (Sullivan 1981).

Catalyst studied practices in 47 companies that offer some kind of flextime work scheduling. The most significant motivator for companies to adopt part-time work, alternate work sites, and job-sharing arrangements was retention of valuable and trained employees. Job-sharing was the least frequently offered arrangement with 32 percent of the 47 companies reporting it; 96 percent reported having a part-time work policy. There were flexible arrangements for professionals across the board. Half of the companies studied had formalized their flexible work schedules or were awaiting approval of one.

Companies surveyed found the benefits of flexible work arrangements to far outweigh their costs. In terms of job-sharing, some human resources professionals felt that it was the most feasible type of work setup because work does not have to be allocated, tasks to be performed on a part-time basis do not have to be identified, and the responsibilities of full-time workers do not have to be reduced. Skills are continually being developed in this arrangement so job sharers are allowed to perform tasks central to the department in which they work.

Catalyst found, in companies with workers on a flexible schedule, that 68 percent of the respondents claimed these arrangements had had a positive effect on retention; 58 percent said they had a positive effect on recruitment as well (or were expected to do so in the future); 70 percent reported enhanced worker morale; and 65 percent said that those working a flexible schedule sustained higher productivity. Flexible work arrangements were also successful in line positions and jobs with supervisory, client, and travel responsibilities.

Stanley Nollen (1980), decrying the traditionally rigid work schedule, said that rather "work tasks come in an infinite variety of sizes (hour-wise) and change continually." He suggests flextime as a means to give workers a measure of autonomy and decision-making "power" by shifting some control to them. Nollen points out that flextime will probably increase productivity, reduce some operating costs, and increase job satisfaction. He infers that it eases the work-family conflict in cases where work schedules and child care arrangements do not mesh.

Flextime became a permanent feature for federal government employees in 1985. Under this plan, an employee may select a starting work time and may modify that schedule with prior notification, a sliding schedule within flexible bands of time is provided, and an employee may vary the length of the work day and week (but must be present during the firm's "core" time)—10:00 A.M. to 3:00 P.M. Credit hours may be carried over, up to 10 hours between pay periods. According to the Bureau of National Affairs (1986), 32 percent of federal employees used the plan.

Although most flexible scheduling programs call for all employees to be at work during a core time, there are three basic programs that allow worker flexibility: employees choose starting and quitting hours to be followed for a limited period; employees can vary starting and quitting times daily; and employees can work more or less than eight hours each day.[9]

The Völvo plant in Köping, Sweden, has adopted multiple shift/flexible work hours to attract people who would ordinarily stay at home, thus maximizing use of the available labor pool. The plan has reduced absenteeism and turnover considerably (Bernstein 1988).

Transamerica Occidental Life Insurance Company of Los Angeles adopted a pilot flextime program in 1973. At present, about 90 percent of the company home office departments participate, including one in Canada. The program was originally used as a recruiting incentive. The rationale behind it was to ease the traffic problem for employees, to give employees a measure of control over their work, and to help solve the child care worry. (The company began a referral service in 1984 and now provides a counseling and information service on child care matters.)

Steelcase, an office furniture manufacturer in Grand Rapids, Michigan, has adopted flextime. The company has 400 of its 2,000 or so office workers participating. Also, 40 office workers share 20 jobs. Flextime policies have reduced absenteeism and the turnover rate, according to Cohn (1988). Since 1988 job-sharing has been offered to the entire workforce. The rationale was the desire to retain the growing number of committed, well-trained employees. Most job sharers at Steelcase are lower level managers or professionals with neither budgetary nor supervisory responsibilities, independent contributors, district sales managers, and employee relations personnel (*Perspective* September, 1989).

A compressed week work schedule is another alternative being tried by some companies. Under this arrangement, an employee can work a 4-day week for 10 hours per day, Monday through Thursday or Tuesday through Friday. This schedule gives a company 2 extra hours a day in which to service its customers, which is especially accommodating to customers located in different time zones. The plan appeals to single parents especially since it gives them a 3-day weekend.

In 1984 Corning, Inc., of Corning, New York, began offering flexible work arrangements on an ad hoc basis to "high performers." The human resource department went formal with the arrangement in 1988 with guidelines that were communicated to all employees. Focus groups made up of 150 salaried employees and managers had input as to how the guidelines were to be communicated. Corning's *Career and Family Book* outlines the comprehensive policies aimed at helping employees balance personal and work responsibilities. Presently, about 35 salaried employees are on a part-time schedule and a few nonexempt employees share jobs (*Perspective* November, 1989).

Eastman Kodak, of Rochester, New York, since November, 1988, allows four kinds of alternative work arrangements: permanent changes in regular, scheduled hours; supervisory flexibility in adjusting daily schedules to accommodate the family needs of employees; temporary and permanent part-time schedules at all levels; and job-sharing.

The law firm of Skadden, Arps, Slate, Meagher, and Flom, of New York City, in 1981 allowed attorneys with two years of experience at the firm to work part-time, an option expanded in 1984 to include new recruits. The expansion recognized the benefits of attracting talented female attorneys. There being a large proportion of female law school graduates (40 percent), it seemed sensible to offer flexible work schedules, according to a company spokesperson.

Using telecommuting as a work setup to fulfill job responsibilities is Pacific Bell's plan for flexible work scheduling.[10] Its telecommuting pilot program began in May, 1985. At the onset, 100 managerial-level volunteers were recruited, and orientation and training sessions were held. Presently, 1,500 of the company's 16,000 salaried employees telecommute; 62 percent work at home one day a week. Increased job satisfaction leading to higher productivity have been reported on the part of a majority of these employees.[11]

FLEXIBLE SPENDING/CAFETERIA ACCOUNT

The first flexible benefits program was established in the early 1970s by TRW; Educational Testing Service followed with a similar program shortly thereafter. The program in both firms was met with enthusiastic response especially since employees had had a hand in structuring the plans.

A cafeteria plan (flexible benefits) comes under the rubric of an employees' welfare plan as defined by Section 3 of the Employment Retirement and Income Security Act. Such a plan is defined as any plan, fund, or program "established and maintained for the purpose of providing . . . medical, surgical, or hospital care or benefits in case of sickness disability, death, unemployment, or vacation benefits . . . training programs, or day care centers, scholarship funds, or prepaid legal services" (Givner 1987). Income deferral and retirement programs come under this rubric as well, as do health care policies for long-term care, which are employer-sponsored.

Other programs include dependent care assistance, vacation time, dependent life insurance, accidental death and dismemberment insurance, dental insurance, 401K plans, and legal aid. Employees can change benefits as needs change. The employee elects, at the beginning of the year, to forego a certain percentage of salary in exchange for the same amount of tax-free contribution for a particular benefit. In the case of dependent care assistance, the employee can use pretax dollars to pay for it up to an amount taken out of a salary. Some pay quarterly, some biweekly.

Employees covered by a cafeteria plan voluntarily accept a pay reduction in exchange for some part or parts of the plan. The savings to employers is that contributions do not subject them to Social Security, unemployment, or state disability obligations. Sometimes these savings alone are enough to cover the plan's administrative costs. Contributions are deductible from employer's gross income as is direct money to employees because benefits are funded by employees' salary reductions. Several developments tend to make a cafeteria benefit plan attractive to employers. Section 25 of the 1978 Revenue Act, as amended in 1980, provides for the selection among cash benefits, taxable and nontaxable benefits, and deferred payments, all embodied in a flexible benefits account.

A full-blown cafeteria plan calls for complete interchangeability among benefits choices and encompasses a benefits account from which one can "draw" benefits or (taxable) cash. At present, the maximum dependent care benefit an employee can elect is five thousand dollars per year. Tax advantages (Social Security, federal income, and often state and local) are ensured by Section 125 of the Internal Revenue Code.[12]

Many people feel that a cafeteria plan is most appropriate for employees with dependent care responsibilities because it represents the full range of circumstances in a diverse work force. Such a plan is gaining in popularity because it addresses individual employees' needs, improves their awareness of available benefits, and has the potential for assuring retention and enhancing productivity (Stonebaker 1984).

Friedman (1986) suggests establishing, as a nontaxable benefit to employees and employers, a dependent care assistance (flexible benefits) plan. To qualify, in the case of the elderly dependent, the elder must be a dependent of the employee for tax purposes, a stipulation that probably explains why relatively few employees take advantage of this type of plan. (Dependency means that the elder is almost totally dependent on a family member.)

It is Stonebaker's (1984) contention that a cafeteria plan should include core, flexible, and incentive components, each with two subcomponents. The core component should embrace those benefits legally mandated and company-provided, which are already part of a company's basic benefits package and subject to eligibility requirements (e.g., tenure). These include income stabilization policies such as Social Security, workman's compensation, and insurance coverage, plus job-loss protection (a measure adopted in 1974 by the Trade Adjustment Assistance Act). The flexible component should be designed with company image vis-à-vis the community and employee satisfaction and identification with the company in mind. Employee self-selection should be its focus, such selection constrained only by time limits on selection and change-of-selection options. Options as part of the flexible component are time off to appear at professional meetings, reimbursement for costs of employment-related activities, relocation, and business travel. The incentive component is one long adopted by many industries and speaks to the productivity level of the company. Benefits include both tangible and intangible rewards for contributions based on the exercise of one's skills and effort, for productivity, and those awarded on the basis of performance appraisal.

Companies vary as to their in-house benefits as part of a flexible account plan. Severance pay agreements, term life and equity insurance benefits, programs to supplement mandated layoff and cutback income, paid time off for national and/or state holidays, vacations, and paid time off for civic activities such as jury and military duties are desirable benefits.

Kamerman and Kahn (1987) discovered a cafeteria benefits-type plan in a high-tech company on the West Coast where 40,000 people are employed, 60 percent of them in a professional capacity. Research and development for the plan began in 1969 to determine what benefits were most appropriate to the workforce and the feasibility of implementing programs. Under the terms of the adopted plan, employees may reassess the program each year as to its application and effectiveness.

In 1978 a pilot flexible benefits plan was introduced to six hundred salaried employees at the American Can Company. (Eventually, the program was extended to all eight thousand salaried employees across the country.) Five benefit areas were addressed: medical, life, vacation, disability, and capital accumulation/retirement. Existing benefits in the five areas were reduced to a minimum level of coverage. The difference in value between existing coverages and the minimum level was "returned" to the employee in the form of flexible credits, which the employee used to "purchase" needed and/or desired optional coverages or to buy back preflexible benefits coverage. Communicating the new program was carried out through meetings, surveys, a hot line, a monthly newsletter, and a "listening post" program. Every year employees indicate their benefits preference for the coming year.

Employees at Pitney Bowes in all cities, as of October 1990, can open a dependent care account for child and elder care. Five thousand dollars per calendar year can be set aside to pay for eligible dependent care expenses on a before-tax basis, the contributions being deducted in equal amounts from paychecks. If both spouses are employed, employees may open an account to pay for eligible dependent care expenses for the care of children under age 13 and of physically or mentally incapacitated dependents. Expenses covered may include a babysitter, parent-elder care, and a nursery school/licensed day care center. Money not used during the calendar year will be forfeited and used to pay for the plan's administrative expenses, unless there is a change in family status during the year. A flexible reimbursement account plan already established for salaried employees of Con Edison in New York City extends to unionized employees on January 1, 1991.

Velleman (1987) reports that the maximum amount of tax-exempt dependent care benefits allowed under Section 125 of the IRS code in the form of a salary reduction has been five thousand dollars a year since 1986. (If any of this amount is not "spent" by the employee, it is "lost.") Section 125 specifies that the amount of salary reduction for dependent care benefits be specified before the beginning of each pay-year and may be altered only in the case of a change in family status. Employees file yearly reports with the IRS, and there are certain nondiscrimination requirements attached to the code. Employee child care assistance is treated as a tax-free benefit for employees; in most cases, employer child care assistance may qualify as a donation and child care benefits are deductible business expenses.

RATIONALE, ADJUSTMENTS, IMPLEMENTATION, FORMS OF RESPONSE

Advantages to implementation of plans and programs to aid working caregivers are numerous and noteworthy. The impact of flexible scheduling, for example, on tardiness, turnover, productivity, overtime costs, and job satisfaction has been studied at various times. Donald J. Peterson (1980) summarizes the impact using results of 11 reported case histories of firms that adopted flextime. The firms represent transportation, manufacturing, banking, insurance, and government. Eight of the eleven firms reported a decrease in absenteeism; in six firms, tardiness was reduced, and eliminated in four. Three of the employers reported significant decreases in overtime costs. Job satisfaction and employee morale were enhanced in seven of the organizations; in nine firms, flextime scheduling was perceived to have had some positive impact on productivity. In some cases, there was an impact of flextiming on productivity through higher worker morale. An advantage of staggered, flexible hours of work is that a firm need not necessarily pay overtime under this arrangement, a utility to a firm that has subsidiaries in other time zones whose schedules must be accommodated. To cope with the possible problem of employees not being supervised under a flextime schedule, Martin and Hartley (1975) suggest staggering supervisory schedules as well as training subordinates to assume some responsibility. Costs involved with rearranged work schedules usually concern communicating the work-schedule change, planning the change by management, and printing periodic memoranda. Ease in commuting and increased productivity were cited as being flextime advantages.

The rationale behind a flextime work schedule is to give workers a choice, though somewhat limited, of when they will work and, thus, more personal freedom. Employees adjust their work hours to fit their personal needs and characteristics. For example, an employee who works better in the early morning will find a 7:00 A.M. to 3:00 P.M. work slot more comfortable than a 9:00 A.M. to 6:00 P.M. schedule. Flextime scheduling is another way for employees to avoid rush-hour traffic, and to be able to conduct one's personal business such as banking during regular business hours. The advantage of a flextime scheduling option to parents with children is to be able to schedule work hours during the time children are in school.[13]

The most significant and important reason for trying a flextime schedule, according to Martin and Hartley (1975), is the easing up of commuting that this schedule permits. In large cities, this is an especially appealing idea. Flextime can thus be seen as one answer to the energy "crisis," because it encourages people to use public transportation (rather than the private automobile) at non-peak hours. Cutting down on private auto usage cuts down on the pollution caused by the starting and stopping of autos in heavy traffic.

The life-cycle of the typical member of the labor force informs us of the attractiveness of a typical flexible benefits-cafeteria program. Marriage and parenthood usually occur from the 20s through the mid-40s; at that time and up until the mid-50s, the last child usually leaves home, creating an "empty nest." It is generally from the early to mid-20s through the mid-50s, then, that home responsibilities and circumstances shift and change, making the option of changing choices of benefits particularly attractive. TRW initiated a project to research the feasibility of a cafeteria benefit plan in late 1969 (Curry 1982), at a time when very little, if anything, was known about how to design, administer, communicate, or fund such a plan. Over four years later, the plan was put into effect. The management policy of TRW at the time took into account the active participation of employees in the decision-making process, a notion that was "friendly" to the development of a viable flexible benefits plan. Compensation for work was considered to include direct pay as well as benefits, and the two were not to be separated conceptually.

Designing the plan involved discovering employees' opinions about the benefits package already in place. This was done through a series of questionnaires. The next step was to determine choices for a revised benefits package. The results revealed a need for a revised package: Nearly all employees chose to change something in their package and expressed satisfaction with the idea that they could manage their total compensation package to fit their individual needs. Management elected to ensure that each employee would have minimum life and hospital/medical coverage. Corporations can cooperate with their local governments and community contacts to press for policy changes in social service offices that would be more accommodating to workers with dependent care responsibilities. Such cooperation could take the form of supporting grants to fund eldercare or child care arrangements. One such arrangement available to elders in the Los Angeles area is houses leased from the city by the Alternative Living for the Aging Agency, which provides households that are surrogates of the conventional family arrangement (Winfield 1987).

Winfield reports a trend to address the dilemma faced by working caregivers of the "new age wave." The trend is a cooperative effort between community consultant groups and businesses to assess a firm's employee caregiving needs and to fashion benefits packages to suit these needs. A private referral service in Massachusetts is being used by IBM to develop the firm's child- and elder-care programs, for example. Workshops have been conducted for PepsiCo, Inc. and Champion International Corporation by the University of Bridgeport's Center for the Study of Aging. Other third party coordinators have been Pathfinders in Scarsdale, New York, and Work and Family Information Directions in Boston. Specifically, in 1986, as a response to the changing demographics of the workforce, IBM, with over 200,000 employees in 50 states, commissioned Work/Family Elder Directions, an organization in Watertown, Massachusetts, to put together an eldercare aid referral service for its employees. The plan, completed in February, 1988, called for directors hired by the firm to develop and staff the service. It is a service to be used by employees, those on leave-of-absence, those receiving benefits under a disability plan, the spouses and surviving spouses eligible for medical benefits, and those with a relative 60 years old or older. No recommendations are made by the counselors; rather, the employee's situation is discussed, needs are determined, available services are described, and names of providers of needed services are offered (Azernoff and Scharlach 1988).

In the first quarter of the plan's existence, it was used twice as much as the company's child care program had been used during its first quarter of operation. In 21 percent of the cases, family stress was cited as the reason for using the service, 32 percent cited "functional difficulties" as the reason and 26 percent gave medical problems as the rationale for using the service. During the first quarter, results of this service were measured. Over 7,000 contacts with providers had been made; more than half of those contacts had resulted in the provision of some service.

A spokesperson for the Lincoln National Life Insurance Company of Fort Wayne, Indiana, relates that their dependent care program to recruit and train day care providers for child care is not only for their 3,400 or so home office employees but for the community as well. Their program has been in existence for five years now. She reports that *Working Woman* magazine has for the past three years listed their program as being "one of the best" of approximately 50 programs of its type. The program, offering comprehensive resource and referral services as well as on-site monitoring of services, has served over 1,500 of the firm's employees to date.

PROBLEMS AND PITFALLS: SUGGESTIONS

Providing workers with caregiver services and implementing these services do not take place without problems and obstacles. Certain procedures need to be followed. No service goes into effect without encountering some kind of resistance, sometimes from upper management, employees themselves, unions, or the community. In any event, the services must be set up with the particular labor pool in mind and workers need to know about the services to maximize their use.

Kamerman and Kahn (1987) suggest that the failure to use available benefits may be caused by lack of access to written information on the company's plan, unclear interpretation of the policies, and the existence of policies that are outdated. Information in the form of bulletins, brochures, and in company newspapers should be provided and "sympathetically" interpreted, according to Kamerman and Kahn. Lane Johnson, personnel manager at Tiernay Metals, a California distribution firm with 133 employees, in an interview with this author, relates how she informs employees of the firm's "wellness" and other benefit-type programs with notices posted on the bulletin board. She feels that employees consult the board with fair frequency, at least to the extent that they know what is available to them.

A lack of responsiveness to the needs of workers can be attributed to an unawareness of demographics concerning the existing labor force and the potential one, unawareness of the range of options available to companies, a reluctance to intrude into employees' private lives, and a narrowly defined corporate social role, according to Helen Axel, director of the Work and Family Information Center of the Conference Board. Lenora Cole Alexander, director of the Women's Bureau of the U.S. Department of Labor, claims that families, employers, local community organizations, communities, and state and federal policymakers should all be responsive to the social concerns of workers. Alexander says that the federal government needs to gather information on what is actually happening with labor in the home setting and then disseminate this information to employers. Incentives for employers to adopt assistance plans are very much needed. In turn, the government can provide funding for startup operations, innovate research about medical programs that can be augmented by private sector industries, provide funding for demonstration projects, and sponsor training programs for dislocated and disadvantaged workers.

Segal (1984) suggests several areas of the work-family dilemma that need attention in these company-sponsored seminars and counseling programs: preventing burn-out, time management, parenting skills, helping children adjust to a working mother and/or father, disciplining children, buildling self-esteem, and making child care work well for all concerned.

With regard to referral services, lack of enough services in the community upon which the firm can draw and to which employees can be referred, or absence of comprehensive programs weaken corporate information and referral abilities. Then, too, child care centers on-site have seldom been found to be the "best" solution to employees' needs for such care. Corporate provision of seed money for area centers is a better mode to attend to this need, according to the Bureau of National Affairs.

Peterson (1980) cautions that certain conditions must exist in an organization for flextime scheduling to be successful. The process of work must be conducive to such scheduling; managers and supervisors must be thoroughly informed of all facets of the scheduling process and operation and must articulate these well. The extent of interdependence of or isolation from other workers among employees are considerations. Peterson urges "proper" administration of the plan with frequent communication about its actual operation among all those involved.

Some restraints on flextime scheduling in certain work settings include those mandated by the Walsh-Healey Act and the Contract Work Standards Act. Both apply to companies holding government contracts worth more than $10,000. Time-and-a-half pay is required in these companies after eight hours of work per day. For workers in interstate commerce, the Fair Labor Standards Act of 1938 requires time-and-a-half pay for weekly hours in excess of 40. Flextime may mean that some employees will have to begin punching a time clock, before- and after-core hours may not be adequately supervised, and the plan itself requires great care in the planning stage. Other drawbacks are that some employees are not at work when their supervisors are, the plan challenges managers with regard to work flow, the existence of timekeeper problems, and the challenge of cross training.

The management of employees on flextime is critical; "self-management" is the key. Peer "policing" of workers and voluntarily generated (not mandated) solutions to problems that arise are germane to an effective flextime scheduled workforce. That supervisors must produce results in the face of disrupted and disjointed work schedules while protecting workers' choices of when to work often becomes a challenge. Herein, there is greater potential for work process breakdown, making the responsibility for coordination even greater. Job redesigning may be called for if flextime is to work cost-effectively.

Flextime scheduling needs to be eased into a benefits system, lest supervisors become overwhelmed by the coming-and-going of employees at erratic hours, seemingly at will. Then, too, it takes time for workers to realize more responsibility for their work and for supervisors to give up some of that responsibility. This may be a problem with personnel who seem to work best under close supervision, with well-specified rules and regulations set upon their work process. Peterson (1980) suggests reviewing the flextime programs in similar firms to learn of the advantages and disadvantages and what type of employees work best under the program. Flextime tends to be best applied to clerical, professional, and managerial workers, but it can be made to work in factory settings with personnel at independent work stations, especially if there is an adequate inventory (Martin and Hartley 1975).

Initially, several apprehensions hindered flexible benefits plans from being widely adopted. First was the notion that such a plan was suited only to special, homogeneous work forces, and not to widely dispersed and heterogeneous employee populations. Another hindrance was the lack of well-staffed, adequately functioning personnel departments and departments capable of working through the legal and design complexities of such plans. The Employment Retirement Income Security Act of 1974 also prohibited benefits under these plans from being part of nontaxable income. The development and implementation of such a plan was often impeded through lack of interest in it until the "last minute" when some kind of coverage was needed immediately.

To properly administer this benefit, election and reimbursement forms must be generated, an account sheet set up for each employee selecting the plan, and the payroll system must reflect and account for taxes withheld.[14]

Finally, any policy or plan can only be as good as the knowledge and handling of it. Educating managers and supervisors in the benefits package, and in the company's interest in it as a means to better the management/worker relationship and achieve a high level of worker satisfaction, is paramount to any implementation. Friedman (1986) has inferred that, even though a company may be committed to a dependent care plan, managers might not be aware of their responsibilities in it or of the company's level of commitment to it.

Managers must be educated about the dependent care problem so that they will be more sensitive and responsible to employees who have these responsibilities. To "match" the project to the needs of a particular work-force, Friedman (1986) allows that it would benefit corporate representatives to serve or sit-in on government proposal review committees to find out about workers' dependent care needs and to check out the feasibility of projects that speak to those needs.

Sensitivity training to inform managers and supervisors of employee family situations is being initiated in some companies, such as the Merck subsidiary in Lawrence, Kansas. Since the inception of awareness training, few complaints about supervisor insensitivity have been heard among the 15,000 employees. Aetna Life and Casualty Company also engages in some awareness training. Having noted in 1987 that 21 percent of their female employees had left technical positions for family reasons and that these women had been better performers than those who had left for other reasons, the company began to focus on informing supervisors and managers about family leave options as well as how to manage job-sharing and part-time work.

Stackel (1986–87) notes that getting the attention of upper management about employees' eldercare responsibilities often prompts companies to address the issue in the first place. These high level managers are in a position to influence policy and initiate solutions. One response to this new awareness was the development of a "self-help for caregivers of the elderly" booklet by Commissioner Carol Frasier Fiske of the Federal Administration on Aging. (Fiske's initiative was the result of her awareness of eldercare commitments among her employees, whose average age was 51.)

Trost (1989a) infers that front-line supervisors and managers can profoundly affect employees' use of a benefit plan. An awareness of changes in the corporate culture as well as a greater sensitivity to the family needs of workers are needed. Problems with "equal" distribution of available benefits arise at times, however. Some managers, for example, especially those with traditional notions of family responsibility and sex roles, may deny some employees the use of the firm's leave benefits. Managers may "play favorites" among employees, catering to higher status employees, or denying the existence of a benefits plan altogether. In certain cases, managers have responded defensively to requests for minimum benefits out of fear that they will lead to "larger" requests.

The costs of implementing infant-child care leave in the public sector have been considered by Frank (1988). When considering costs, three criteria must be considered: eligibility, wage and benefit levels, and length of leave. Eligibility criteria include the length of time on the job and some productivity standard. Three rates of wage-salary compensation during leave are suggested: 100 percent, 75 percent, and 50 percent. The length of leave time allowance should take into consideration the physical and emotional needs of the family and the loss of productivity to employers and the public. The expense of training replacements in the absence of a leave policy, should the employee not return, should be part of the calculation. At any rate, whoever or whatever finances leave-taking (the employer, the employee, the government, or a combination), employee and employer should not have to suffer a disproportionate effect of leave-taking. Nor should the financing create unintended economic "incentives" that would discourage employers from hiring women, the most frequent leave-takers.

With job-sharing, benefits can be problematic. If benefits are awarded according to the number of hours worked, these jobs accrue fewer benefits, making them potentially exploitative. Yet, giving full benefits to part-time workers is a disincentive to employers to make these jobs more available.

THE "BEST"

What does the "score card" look like in the area of care benefits? *Working Mother* magazine mailed questionnaires to several hundred U.S. companies to determine the "best" ones for working mothers' needs. Four categories were rated: pay compared with competitors; opportunities for advancement; support for child care, maternity and parental leaves, adoption aid, flextime, part-time work, and job-sharing; and support for employees with eldercare responsibilities.[15] Sixty companies were chosen as the best. The top ten included:

1. Apple Computer in California, which operates an on-site child care center in which 70 are enrolled and which has a flexible benefits plan (among others).

2. Beth Israel Hospital of Boston with a referral service, liberal maternity leave, and priority access to a nearby center.

3. DuPont, which funds child care centers, has a pretax salary set-aside plan, maternity leave, flextime, and job-sharing.

4. Fel-Pro of Skokie, Illinois.

5. Hoffman-LaRoche of Nutley, New Jersey.

6. IBM of Armonk, New York.

7. Merck of Rahway, New Jersey, which offers the services of a nearby center, has a referral service, maternity and parental leave, flextime, and job-sharing.

8. The law firm of Morrison and Foerster of San Francisco, offering a pretax salary set-aside plan, paid sick leave to care for an ill child, maternity and parental leave, flex- and part-time work, and job-sharing.

9. The nation's leading producer of computer software products, SAS Institute of Cary, North Carolina.

10. Syntex of Palo Alto, California, offering a near-site care center, pretax salary set-aside, maternity leave, part-time hours, job-sharing, and adoption aid.

It should be noted that many companies have taken up the torch for the benefit of workers' home/work dilemma, a dilemma very much a part of many workers' lives. The dilemma is being addressed in a variety of ways through human resource and personnel offices. Yet, impediments to addressing these issues remain—especially the traditional sex role stereotypes we hold.

Coontz (1989) speaks indirectly to the notion of traditional sex role stereotypes and views of the "proper" structure of a family as clouding the real issues behind family needs and poverty. Her arguments infer that these traditions often stand in the way of some corporate policymakers' recognition of workers' family concerns. To more fairly distribute worker benefits, then, corporate officers may need to update their views of women's and men's "proper" roles. "Proper," today, should refer to what works best and what is functional for all concerned. "Proper" may not necessarily mean wives going to work and other nontradition-locked family practices, but rather economic and political transformations that are directly linked to family poverty. But pro-family notions about traditional sex roles tend to cloud the real issues, such as what programs and practices are most supportive to family practices now in effect. We can no longer fail to see that women of all ages are in the labor force to stay. Motivations for being there should not determine what kinds of accommodations should be made to keep them there and to maintain them as productive workers. The notion of what is "proper," then, in the old sense, no longer is valid in an age when the United States is trying to regain its productivity edge by making physical and human capital more productive.

NOTES

1. Dependent care assistance plans are required to pass a "nondiscrimination" test designed to ensure that highly compensated employees such as managers do not receive tax-favored benefits that are significantly more generous than those provided to employees of different rank. At Con Edison in New York City in 1989, a highly compensated employee was one with an annual compensation of at least $54,480, a number that was indexed to inflation and adjusts each year.

2. A study by the Catalyst (1986a) group revealed that the most frequently favored dependent care options companies reported, in order of frequency, were child care information services, flexible working hours, flexible benefits with a child care option, a salary reduction plan creating pretax dollars for child care, job-sharing, and seminars at the workplace. The option least favored was subsidies for child care and on- or near-site child care centers.

3. Subjects in this study, all women, cared for elderly parents in the Merrimack Valley of Massachusetts (see Gibeau et al. 1987).

4. Another project that eventually was phased out existed at Equitable Life Assurance of Atlanta. Subsidizing slots for children at local day care facilities and guaranteeing payment for a certain number of spaces in the local centers was the format.

5. From a parental leave policies study begun in 1983, funded by Revlon Foundation, Inc., Catalyst (1986b) found that companies had little knowledge about the leave-related needs of their employees. Few had access to data on employees' needs that would have allowed them to review and revise existing policy and few acknowledged parental leave policies as a tool to recruit and retain workers.

6. A disability leave provision is not common in very small companies. In one study reported by Sheinberg (1988), 37 percent of companies with between 50 and 100 employees had such a policy, whereas only 10 percent of those with fewer than 10 had such a policy.

7. Hiring temporaries from outside the company often generates the problem of lost productivity due to inexperience on the part of the temporary workers.

8. The Caregivers in the Workplace materials can be obtained by contacting AARP, P.O. Box 19269—Station R, Washington, DC 20036.

9. Flexible scheduling works best for sales personnel, some technicians, natural scientists, insurance and real estate personnel, finance personnel, mathematical and computer scientists, and workers in personal services. The five-day, 40-hour week schedule became standard at the end of World War II; rearranging work week schedules began in the 1960s in the United States.

10. Telecommuting involves an electronic mailing system of data entered on one computer transferred electronically to another computer. It alleviates unnecessary time off, among other things (McGee 1988), reduces turnover, and improves morale and productivity (Eskow 1989).

11. The formulation of effective flextime programs, according to Catalyst, is best done by first consulting the company's legal department for advice on avoiding discrimination, appointing a human resource professional to coordinate and monitor the program, and providing an inclusive communication means, perhaps with a handbook.

12. See Velleman (1987) for a concise explanation of the plan's specifications.

13. Flextime scheduling is not *necessarily* appropriate in assembly line or machine-paced work, although it has been tried successfully in Sweden in these types of settings.

14. One of the benefits to employers of a cafeteria plan is the possible FICA tax savings because the amount of benefits paid to employees is tax exempt.

15. Moskowitz and Townsend (1989) authored the article in *Working Mother*. The benefits plans of many more companies other than the top 10 are also described.

4

A Survey of Dependent Care Policies

An interpretation of data from a mailed survey questionnaire is the topic of this chapter. Many studies have been conducted to determine the availability of dependent care assistance and the types of policies available not only to the general public but specifically to members of the formal labor force. The study reported on here perhaps differs in no significant ways from most of the others. However, this study was conducted at a time when, more than ever, business owners were being made aware of what some viewed as a threat to their autonomy in terms of how to compensate employees. For instance, the U.S. Chamber of Commerce had sent out a flyer to businesses asking them to protest dependent care legislation that would, seemingly, threaten the capability of private companies to initiate their own policies specific to their particular workforces. The flyer was sent out at a time when employees at companies and legislative bodies were agitating for some kind of assistance programs aimed at helping workers with dependent care responsibilities.

New Medicare and Medicaid provisions went into effect in January of 1989, liberalizing in several ways the provisions. An article in the Colorado Springs *Gazette Telegraph* of November 22, 1989, informs us that the House rejected a last-ditch proposal to salvage some catastrophic medical benefits for older Americans, assuring repeal of the entire program. All that remained was for the Senate to agree to the repeal and send the measures to the president for his signature. The House had voted earlier in the day for repeal by a 352 to 63 margin. The Senate then proposed to kill the surtax part of the benefit and repeal extended Medicare benefits for doctor bills and prescriptions, but keep most of the expansion of hospital coverage provided by the catastrophic measure. The House had found unacceptable the reduced hospital coverage and a package of minor benefits, including home health care, financed by a monthly premium that would not have risen above six dollars.

In the spring of 1989, AT&T and its unions signed a contract specifying liberal dependent care benefits to workers. The contract was termed "innovative." In the fall of 1989, more was heard about a fairly innovative child care plan encompassing means to attend to sick children so that their parents would not miss work. Many of the 173 respondents to my survey indicated future commitments on the part of their companies to install dependent care policies and plans. There are perhaps no definitive flashpoints in the emergence of dependent care assistance for workers, but it does seem that one can hardly pick up a newspaper or a national magazine in which the dependent care "problem" and its incumbent issues are not at least referred to indirectly. For these reasons and others, the survey described here is timely.

THE SURVEY

Using a systematic selection technique, 302 companies were taken from a list of names of 796 executives of U.S. companies, published in the April 25, 1988, issue of *Forbes* magazine. Fifty-seven percent (N = 173) of the companies surveyed responded to the questionnaire, which was mailed in February, 1989.

The types of companies surveyed were financial institutions, insurance firms, wholesale-retail firms, utilities companies, manufacturing firms, service companies, pharmaceutical and medical businesses, and technological/electronic/aerospace/energy companies. They were placed in nine size-of-labor-force categories and represented four broad regions of the country: the Northeast, Midwest, South, and West including Hawaii.[1]

Those types of policies identified were a flexible benefits and spending account/cafeteria plan, a referral facility or service, an on-site center, an off-site center, a consortium plan by which several firms maintain a center,

a public/private partnership by which a firm commits funds to be used for local care and referral agencies, and "other."

Fifty-six percent (N = 35) of the firms in the Northeast reported a policy, as did those in the West (N = 14). Fifty-three percent in the Midwest claimed to have a policy, whereas 43 percent in the South did so, making the South the area containing the largest proportion of the respondents without a policy. (See Figure 4.1.)

In all four regions, the type of policy most likely to have been adopted was a flexible spending account/cafeteria plan for child care followed by the same plan for elder care. A referral service for child care was the next most popular form of dependent care assistance. Job-sharing was specified in one company in the Northeast; two northeastern companies reported an off-site child care center, one being in a pharmaceutical firm. Two on-site care centers were reported in companies in the West, and one in the Midwest, all at financial services industries. The midwestern firm reports

Figure 4.1
Region by Yes and No Responses

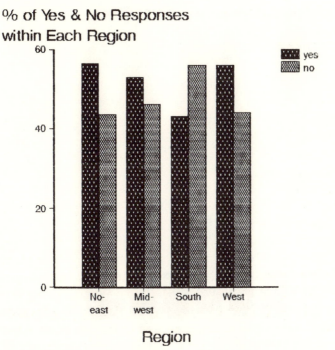

extensive use of the center. Other types of policies and programs were part-time work, seminars, pretax vouchers, discounted day care arrangements, partnerships, donations to public organizations, parental leave, and flextime.

Those firms most likely to report having dependent care policies have from 1,100 to 5,000 employees (44 percent of those with a policy); those next most likely are those with 5,100 to 15,000 employees (23 percent of those with a policy). Those with 15,100 to 30,000 employees were the next most likely to have a policy (10 percent), and 9 percent of those with a policy have from 100 to 1,000 employees. Those least likely to report a policy have from 60,100 to 75,000 employees followed by those with 75,100 to 90,000 employees (less than 1 percent of those with a policy). In total, nearly 54 percent (N = 93) of the respondents claimed to have some kind of dependent care assistance policy. These data appear in Figure 4.2.

According to Sheinberg (1988), in general, larger firms have more resources and are therefore more generous in providing employee benefits

Figure 4.2
Size of Company Having At Least One Policy

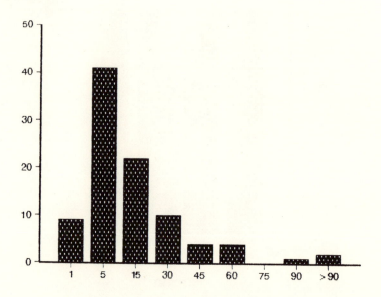

Responses

Size in Thousands of Employees

than are smaller firms. My findings generally do not bear out this, probably because I did not use the same size classification as Sheinberg. In fact, it was the very large companies (those with 15,100 employees or more) that were the least likely to report dependent care assistance. Sheinberg maintains that larger companies are usually trendsetters and looking for ways to gain a competitive edge over others in their industry. A benefits policy can act as a tool for job-enhancement; it can serve as a model for the industry as a whole in attracting highly qualified personnel. Where one leads, others are likely to follow is the rationale.

Reported usage of existing policies and programs was examined in this survey. Moderate usage was the pattern for the largest proportion of firms, followed by an infrequent pattern. Only five firms with a child care referral plan reported extensive usage; two with a flexible spending account/cafeteria plan for child care reported extensive use; three with a child and eldercare referral plan did so. Far more businesses reported very little or infrequent usage than reported extensive usage in all size categories of firms.

Table 4.1
Type of Policy by Usage

	Very little	Moderate	Extensively
Flexible-child	11	30	2
Flexible-elder	14	30	3
Referral-child	4	23	5
Referral-elder	6	7	1
On-site center	1	2	1
Off-site center	1	3	1
Partnership-child	0	3	1
Partnership-child/elder	1	1	0

Given that the most frequently reported use of companies' plans and policies is moderate, we find that flexible spending for both child and eldercare, and referral services for child and elder assistance are most frequently used on a moderate basis rather than very little or extensively (See Table 4.1). The next most frequently reported mode of use for both child and eldercare flexible accounts was "very little." Referral services for child care assistance were used equally "very little" and "extensively." On-site and off-site care centers and partnerships are faring better, with companies reporting *at least* moderate use of these services by employees.

Thirty-six of the respondents that reported a policy were financial institutions; thirteen were manufacturing firms. Utilities firms and technological/electronic/aerospace/energy companies were equally as likely to report having policies (12 of each of these two types of firms reporting policies), as were service and pharmaceutical and medical businesses (4 in each case reported policies). Manufacturing firms were the most likely to report the absence of a policy, followed by financial firms (22 and 18, respectively). Insurance firms were the least likely of all types of firms to report not having a policy; three such firms reported having such a policy (See Table 4.2.)

Seventy-seven percent of the financial services firms and 88 percent of the wholesale-retail firms report a flexible spending-cafeteria plan for child care assistance; 58 percent and 33 percent, respectively, have this plan for

Table 4.2
Type of Firm by Yes and No Responses

Type	Yes	No
Financial	36	18
Whole/Retail	9	10
Tech/Elect	12	13
Utility	12	11
Service	4	3
Manufacturing	13	22
Pharm/Medical	4	2
Insurance	3	1
Total	93	80

eldercare assistance. All the respondent technology/electronics/aerospace/ energy firms, pharmaceutical-medical, and insurance companies have this type of plan for child care assistance. In all types of firms, with respect to flexible spending and referral plans, elder care assistance is not available to the same extent as child care assistance, except in insurance firms where assistance for both is equal. In no service business was there a flexible account for eldercare, and in manufacturing firms there was no referral service for eldercare assistance. One insurance company has a referral service for child care assistance.

Firms reporting extensive use of their dependent care assistance programs are service, financial, electronics, manufacturing, utilities, and retail companies. Data pertaining to the extent of usage of plans and policies by the size of firms reveal that the largest number of firms reporting moderate use had 1,100 to 5,000 employees, followed by those with 5,100 to 15,000 employees. Those firms reporting extensive use of policies and plans are companies with 5,100 to 15,000 employees on the payroll, followed by those with 1,100 to 5,000 employees.[2] Firms with 1,100 to 5,000 and 5,100 to 15,000 employees were about equal in reporting policy use as very little. Firms with 45,100 to 60,000 employees were more likely than any others to report *at least* moderate use of their dependent care policies. (See Figure 4.3.)

One reason why pretax dollar plans are being used only moderately may be the reluctance of caregivers to whom these dollars are paid to acknowledge caregiving because of the tax and licensing ramifications. A spokesperson for a New York State utilities company, wishing to remain anonymous, reported that in 1989 only 17 percent of the firm's large workforce had taken advantage of the child care pretax voucher portion of the flexible benefits plan on board. According to the spokesperson, this number of users may possibly decrease because of the IRS stipulation that an employee taking a pretax benefit for child care must report the name and address of the child caregiver that went into effect in 1989. It could also increase the cost of child care as providers heretofore unlicensed, in order to maintain a clientele, will have to become licensed, a procedure that is costly.[3] Then, too, imposing more red tape on providers by the IRS and prosecuting those without a license may force many out of business, making the job of finding proper child care services more difficult. Regulations and reduced competition, in turn, would drive up prices for care. Licensing is supposed to control, to an extent, quality of care, but this could just as well be done by a Department of Social Services by publishing health and safety guidelines for day care. It would, thus, be up

Figure 4.3
Size of Firm by Usage

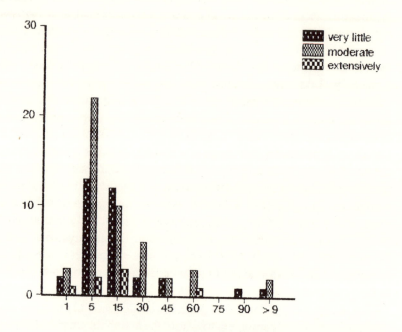

Usage

Size in Thousands of
Employees

to the user of services to determine the desireability of any service and facility.

The extent of job-sharing and flextime scheduling was not determined in this study but were mentioned as available options by several firms. Job-sharing has been offered, since April of 1989, at an eye care products manufacturing firm in New York State. A social service company in North Carolina offers reduced work hours allowing time away from work to care for dependents.

According to a Catalyst study (1986a), flexible work schedules are more likely to be in companies in the West; child care information services are more likely to be located in companies in the Northeast, as is monetary support of community child care. These findings concur, in a manner of speaking, with the findings of my survey: those firms most likely to report having some kind of assistance policy are located in the West and Northeast. According to the Catalyst study, firms allowing sick days for children's illnesses were located in the South and the West.

With some of the respondents, certain benefits are available only to management and not to union and certain other employees. Such is the case with a utilities firm where its flexible reimbursement account plan for health care and dependent care expenses are available to about 6,000 management employees (out of a workforce of 20,000). The firm's referral facility for child care assistance is available to all employees, however. This firm is in a partnership whereby it has committed funds to be used for local care and referral agencies servicing employees for child and eldercare assistance. A communications service industry in Colorado, considered to be in the forefront of dependent care assistance to its employees, has a flexible benefits and spending account and a referral facility available to a portion of its workforce only.

CASE STUDIES AND INITIATIVES

Private sector initiative on behalf of employees with dependent care responsibilities is evident from my survey. Several respondent companies noted that certain benefits plans are forthcoming. An energy firm in Ohio, for example, with a payroll of 9,000, planned to implement a cafeteria plan for the benefit of child care in January of 1990. A pharmaceutical firm in New Jersey has future plans to establish an off-site child care center and a flexible benefits and spending account for child care. Referral services also are being considered by this company.

A spokesperson for a respondent financial service firm, in a telephone interview, spoke of the rationale behind the company's cafeteria-spending account "125 plan" for employees, 70 percent of whom are women. Given the changing demographics affecting the family, the firm allowed employees to customize their benefits according to their particular needs. Employees who chose this account can set aside a maximum of $5,000 in pretax dollars a year for health care services and/or day care services for both children, elders, and other dependents. Employees can "mix" benefits.

A spokesperson at U.S. West, a company with about 60,000 employees in some 14 states, told of a near-site child care center it cosponsors with America West Airlines in Tempe, Arizona. The center has been operating for 1 1/2 years. The company is recognizing that family care issues are caregiver issues, rather than child or eldercare issues, and is responding to this perception. It plans to add to its already existing referral and resource plan for child care, a plan for eldercare. U.S. West also offers flexible working arrangements to include telecommuting, job-sharing, and compressed work weeks.

A spokesperson for a utilities company in New York State reported on its 2 1/2-year-old before-tax child care compensation plan. The rationale behind the adoption of this plan was simply that legislation allowed it and that it would benefit the workers who were parents. This plan seemed more appropriate to employee's needs as compared to a child care center because most employees seemed to be at least somewhat satisfied with their own child care arrangements. The company now is considering the adoption of a flexible spending account plan for medical expenses for employees' dependents.

A software manufacturer in California with 2,100 employees is developing a proposal for a dependent care program. A financial service in Washington with a flexible benefits plan already implemented has a referral service pending. A financial service company in Colorado with 3,000 employees in 43 banks statewide conducted a dependent care needs assessment early in 1989 and was in the process of considering such dependent care assistance options as a flexible spending account, referral services, a partnership, off- and on-site care centers, and a consortium plan. Another financial service in California is currently researching dependent care assistance options for its 765 employees. Another financial firm implemented a child care referral service in March, 1989. (A manufacturing company in Michigan recently surveyed all employees with children under the age of 13 to identify child care needs.) A retail firm in Minnesota is planning to include a referral service for eldercare as part of its child care referral service. As yet, the firm offers a "very limited" flexible benefits account and referral service for child care assistance.

A technology company in Connecticut with 110,000 employees across the country planned a flexible benefits and spending account for eldercare assistance for January 1990. A telecommunications business in Illinois recently began doing the same. A computer firm in Massachusetts has pending a referral service for both child care and eldercare assistance. At the corporate office of a retail company in Ohio, a pretax dollar account plan for dependent care assistance is in its first year of operation. A banking industry firm has a flexible benefits and spending account "in progress" and reports that a consortium plan feasibility study had been underway when a franchised day care firm opened a facility instead. A survey of employees' need for a care center revealed that an on-site center at one location was not a practical plan.

Con Edison of New York, an electric utility and one of the respondent companies, offers comprehensive child care and eldercare services as well as an emergency child care plan for management employees. A resource guide to include telephone numbers of senior and health services is part of the service. An information and referral service packet for employees describes Con Ed's not-for-profit program called Child Care, Inc., founded in 1969 to provide services for parents in the five boroughs of New York City. For the past six years, this organization has provided counseling services for employees of major businesses in the city. The service is funded through corporate memberships, foundation grants, and individual contributions and fees for services.

Child Care, Inc. coordinates a network of 15 child care information and referral agencies in the New York metropolitan area, providing initial consultation by telephone, and arranges with the appropriate agency to contact the person making the request with information on child care in the individual's community. Information on how to evaluate programs and how to find the best provider is given also.

The company has on board a flexible reimbursement account and adoption benefit plan, provides both salaried and unionized employees parental leave that includes pregnancy-related leave-of-absence before and/ or after childbirth, and sick absences under the company's sick allowance procedures. Child care leaves are also granted, are unpaid, and offered for birth and adoption to both parents. Both types of leaves may be granted for up to 90 days with an extension allowed by request for a total of 180 days. If leave is requested and granted beyond that period, reinstatement is not guaranteed beyond the 180 days. The company pays the full cost of unionized employee health benefits for up to three months during a leave of absence immediately following the employee's maternity disability.

Con Edison also provides a handbook on eldercare, which includes information on how to find the best resources to meet the needs of elderly dependents. A flexible reimbursement account plan allows salaried employees to pay dependent care costs of up to $5,000 a year with before-tax dollars. Elderly dependents who are physically or mentally disabled and unable to care for themselves are covered under this arrangement.

SUMMARY

The most popular type of dependent care assistance policy from the survey seems to be a flexible spending account/cafeteria plan for at least child care assistance. Workers who are caregivers of the elderly are getting less assistance from their employers than caregivers of children because there are fewer companies with eldercare assistance plans. A referral service for help with child care is the next most frequently offered assistance for employees. This service for eldercare assistance is present to a lesser extent in respondent firms.

Companies are beginning to take the initiative in establishing on- and off-site care centers: four have on-site centers, five are involved in off-site centers. Partnerships, flextime, parental leave, and a discounted day care arrangement were other modes of assistance indicated. These modes were most present in financial institutions and least present in manufacturing firms. Companies with 1,100 to 5,000 employees were the most likely to report having at least one dependent care assistance policy, and these companies were most likely to be located in the northeastern and western regions of the country.

This survey did not inquire about parental leave, and only two companies mentioned this benefit in the "other" category. Parental leave legislation, however, is pending at the federal level.

NOTES

1. Size categories were: 100 to 1,000; 1,100 to 5,000; 5,100 to 15,000; 15,100 to 30,000; 30,100 to 45,000; 45,100 to 60,000; 60,100 to 75,000; 75,100 to 90,000, and larger than 90,000 employees.

2. The definition of a large, medium, and small firm differs according to several variables, one being the region of the country in which the firm is located. For purposes of this study, however, those firms with 1,100 to 15,000 employees are considered to be medium to large.

3. It has been estimated that there are 1.7 million unlicensed neighborhood day care providers caring for three-quarters of the children in day care facilities (*Gazette Telegraph* Nov 7, 1989).

5

Future Prospects for Dependent Care Assistance

This chapter examines what dependent care policies and programs may look like in the future in light of what is happening to them now. Trends are suggested by the changes in the ways dependent care policies such as parental leave are being viewed and in the activities on the part of employers both public and private on behalf of dependent care assistance. Child care issues as well as those involving the long-term care needs of the elderly are being regarded as top priority concerns for the 1990s. Legislation is pending, and the private sector is jumping on the dependent care bandwagon; future prospects for dependent care for working families look good.

The number of companies offering help with the dependent care burden increased more than 500 percent between 1982 and 1989. Results from a 1988 survey of 521 large corporations by the Conference Board in New York City revealed that 90 percent of the respondents offer part-time employment and 22 percent offer job-sharing (often at reduced salaries) as an arrangement. Fifty percent allowed flextime scheduling (Nyborg-Andersen and O'Brien 1989). Results from my survey indicate that over 50 percent of the respondents claimed at least a referral service for child care. A study conducted by the Bureau of National Affairs in 1986, based on the premise that corporate America has not kept pace with the changing dynamics between work and family, revealed that although only 23 percent of the firms surveyed made allowances for taking personal leave, a full 77 percent offered leave without pay.

The American Federation of State, County, and Municipal Employees organization (AFSCME) conducted a study of contracts of its members in 1987 and discovered that 72 percent provided for maternity or parental leave, whereas over half provided the right to leave for periods of, or exceeding, four months. Increasingly men were included in parental leave coverage. Fathers' involvement, or at least interest, in the child care issue may be increasing. Presently, an estimated 14 percent of dads are "watching after" their preschoolers (Nyborg-Andersen and O'Brien 1989). Companies doing studies in this area find an increasing interest on the part of men in child-raising issues, partially because of the number of fathers who are single parents.

However, parental leave-taking by men may not yet be the norm. The Catalyst Career and Family Center of New York City received responses from 384 of *Fortune* magazine's 1,500 companies to a survey regarding benefits such as leaves and job guarantee. Only nine companies of the 37 percent providing unpaid, job-guaranteed leave to men reported that male employees had taken such leave. Only 37.2 percent of the companies providing paternity leave considered it appropriate for men to take it.

The trend in dependent care assistance has been set, however. Who gets there first with the most—private or public sector—remains to be seen. Indications are that dependent care concerns are receiving national attention and, in terms of our labor force, are emerging as a top priority issue. Awareness not only of the present emerging demographics but of what ensues from them will be the foundation upon which greater responsiveness to the family-work conflict will be and is being made. There is also greater public awareness of these concerns. For example, a survey sponsored by AARP (Carlson 1990) indicates Americans would strongly support a government-sponsored plan to provide citizens of all ages with some form of in-home and nursing home care. This attitude was found to be consistent across all age groups, and reflects the extent to which the long-term care issue concerns Americans. The survey revealed that nearly two-thirds of those polled are "very concerned" about the cost of long-term care, and more than half are "not very" or "not at all" confident that they would be able to pay for long-term care. Two-thirds of those polled said they had direct or indirect experience with the problems of providing long-term care.

We can hardly avoid encountering what is being written about dependent care—in women's magazines, *The Wall Street Journal, U.S. News and World Report*, the *New York Times*, as well as in the more specialized and narrowly focused publications. It's an issue of the 1990s, according to the *Kiplinger Washington Letter* of April 7, 1989, which forecasts continuing state regulation of business in the area of unpaid leave. The *Letter* predicted that states eventually will require businesses to allow unpaid leave for either parent with job reinstatement assured.

Fierman (1988) notes that in 1988 over one hundred dependent care bills confronted Congress, and although none passed the legislative body, the issue is far from dead. Labor Secretary (in the Reagan administration) Ann McLaughlin is quoted as saying that child care is *the* challenge to society for the 1990s. Givner (1987) allows that although some dependent care plans have some weaknesses in terms of their "safety" value, it is the "hot topic" in employee benefits at present. Pending in the 101st Congress as of February, 1990, is the matter of long-term care policies. The Pepper Commission on Health Care headed by Senator John D. Rockefeller IV (D-WV) is spearheading a study aimed at developing a comprehensive health plan including a long-term care system. Senate Majority Leader George Mitchell (D-ME) claims he will reintroduce a long-term care bill, and Representative Pete Clark (D-CA) has introduced a bill restoring four benefits from the rescinded catastrophic measures such as respite care and liberalized hospice care support.

The need for child care services could well be the priority among priorities for the 1990s. This theme was supported by an article in the Colorado Springs *Gazette Telegraph* issue of September 1, 1989, reporting survey results from 278 of the country's largest cities. Results indicated that quality, affordable day care programs are a most pressing public need now. (The survey was conducted by the National League of Cities.) Sixty-three percent of the respondents ranked child care for infants up to two, 80 percent for children two to five, and 69 percent for children five to nine, as the number-one issue, according to James Moran, the League's Human Development Policy Committee chairman.

Dependent care needs are becoming an important issue not only because of the legislative and business consideration afforded them, but because of the cost to taxpayers of not having dependent care services to workers. Dr. Heidi Hartmann of the Institute for Women's Policy Research estimated the cost of the lack of national parental leave policies. Compared to new mothers with parental leave allowances, taxpayers pay $715 million a year in the form of assistance for the lack of leave for childbearing and rearing.

We may well see in the future more cooperation and functional and mutual "reinforcement" between state and private entities with a symmetrical flow of influence where dependent care needs are concerned. For example, although very few studies have been conducted to determine the impact on businesses of having family and medical leave policies, a study by the 9to5 National Association of Working Women indicated that small business employment did better in states that have some form of parental leave policies mandated than it did in states without these policies. (Information from the Small Business Administration on private sector employment says that seven of 21 states having parental leave policies in 1986 were California, Colorado, Connecticut, Kansas, Massachusetts, Montana, and Washington.) Businesses located in the states with parental leave policies grew at a rate of 21 percent more than small businesses in states without such policies. It would seem, further, that employment growth itself gets a boost in businesses located in parental leave states. In firms with fewer than 20 employees, employment grew by 32 percent in companies in parental leave policy states compared to 22 percent in businesses in nonparental leave states.

States are offering tax credits to businesses for child care assistance, according to Trost (1980b). There is growing support for these credits among legislators because of the low-cost, easy-to-implement way they use limited public funds to urge private sector involvement in the child care issue. Under this plan, employers reduce, dollar for dollar, the state taxes they owe.

With regard to maternity leave, probably their allowance will continue to vary by the nature and size of a particular firm. The larger the company, the more likely one is to find eligibility for maternity leave with re-employment rights and eligibility for maternity leave with pay. And the larger the company, the more likely maternity leave will be given to new employees. Granting of maternity leave will continue to be less likely in wholesale and retail trade and nonprofessional service industries.

THE GOVERNMENT AND DEPENDENT CARE

The government's involvement in dependent care issues is found in the breaks to industry that are given for setting up and operating child care programs.[1] Employers in California, until 1991, can get a 30 percent credit of up to $30,000 for the cost of establishing a care program or facility for children, and a 50 percent credit of up to $600 per year per employee for the operating costs of the program or facility. In 1988, 22 states offered 10 to

25 percent breaks to offset some dependent care costs. Other states allow deductions or credits based on expenses and personal benefits ranging from $75 per year to $150 per year in some states. At present, five states (those in which 23 percent of all workers live) require all employers to provide short-term disability plans or subscribe to a state plan. Only 2.4 percent of all employees are affected by state laws that require parental leave, however.

Massachusetts, New Jersey, and Pennsylvania have increased state funding to provide affordable child care and increased wages for child caregivers. So have North Carolina and Ohio; they have also increased their day care licensing capacities and ability to respond to reports of abuse by caregivers. In Iowa and New Jersey, money has been designated to set up resource and referral services. California provides child care for children of welfare recipients and welfare parents participating in job training and placement programs. As of 1987 seven states provided funds to schools to provide before- and after-school care for students. Preschool programs in schools are being initiated in approximately 19 states. These programs vary somewhat by state in their comprehensiveness, however.

Dependent care was addressed by the Economic Equity Act of 1989. Introduced in June, the EEA is an omnibus measure comprising 23 bills that address a range of issues confronting families. The first EEA was developed by the Congresswomen's Caucus and introduced into the 97th Congress in 1981. Past EEA successes include the passage of a child care provision within the Higher Education Amendments of 1986. EEA is expected to send a strong message to lawmakers that economic improvement is crucial and requires a multifaceted response to the changing demographics and to the diverse needs of families. By addressing a broad range of economic issues, the bill attracts broad bipartisan congressional support (*Outlook*, 1989).

Under this measure, states would be helped to subsidize day care costs for children under 13 for those families with incomes under a standard set by each state. The proposal would provide $500 million in grants to help states improve and expand child care facilities, would expand the existing dependent care tax credit to 34 percent for poor families, and would refund existing dependent care tax credits if no taxes are owed. The Republican version would expand the earned income tax credit for families with children under five years old, and provide up to $500 credit for the first child and up to $250 for a second child. Low income families would not have to enroll their children in a day care facility to be eligible. The measure would refund the existing 30 percent dependent care tax credit if no taxes are owed and provide $400 million to states to assist in providing child care services. For Social Security recipients, child care earnings from the outside earnings limitations would be exempt.[2]

The basis for child care support began in 1942 with the Lantham Act. Rescinded at the end of World War II, it provided grants to states to support care for children of working mothers. In 1971 child care legislation was proposed in the Nixon administration but vetoed by the president. In 1976 a flat rate of tax credit for families in which there were children under 13 was enacted. The measure was expanded in 1981, with more generous allowances to low income households allowed. Such households were allowed a 30 percent credit for expenditures up to $2,400 for those with incomes of $10,000 or less.

In 1974 a block grant under Title XX of the Social Security Act gave grants to states to provide services for those on welfare. Two billion dollars of original appropriation were to have been set aside for child care under this measure. The 1980s saw some reductions in past measures: federal interagency day care requirements were suspended—these had allowed the federal government a role in monitoring the quality of day care provided; Title XX funds were reduced; and funding for child care services was no longer earmarked. These funds were reduced further in March, 1986.

We are beginning to see more activity from the public sector with regard to the growing U.S. elderly population as well. The federal government's activities on behalf of the elderly emanated from the Older Americans Act of 1965. This act eventually created 57 area agencies on aging in the country. Agencies are required to provide referral services, transportation, home health aid, and legal aid services to the elderly. Attendants such as housekeepers and homemakers and home health aides are to be made available from $6 to $9 an hour. The annual budget for the agencies is between $35 and $40 million.

The government-elderly-business connection is seen in a provision in the IRS code. Section 129 of this code makes eldercare expenses nontaxable to employees and employers, and permits the inclusion of eldercare programs in a flexible benefits plan called a dependent care assistance plan (Friedman 1986).

MEDICARE

Changes in the Medicare program will probably continue as more people draw benefits and the needs of those over 85 become more pressing. Medicare legislation has an interesting history, beginning in 1915 when

academics, lawyers, and other professionals organized as the American Association for Labor Legislation. From the beginning, any attempts to "socialize" medical care were met with opposition from the medical community, mainly by the American Medical Association (AMA). When a model medical care insurance bill was introduced early on, it failed to pass several state legislatures because of this opposition as well as that of labor representatives who feared it would herald government control over workers.

Opposition to national health insurance was formulated around the notions that this insurance was a giveaway program that did not distinguish between the truly needy and the nonneedy, that it would swell the utilization of existing medical services beyond their capacity, that it comprised excessive federal control of physicians, and that physicians would refuse to provide requested services. Along with the AMA, the American Hospital Association, the National Association of Manufacturers, the American Legion, and the Chambers of Commerce opposed Medicare legislation as it was proposed.

During Franklin Roosevelt's New Deal era in the 1930s, government-sponsored health insurance was not vigorously endorsed because such a program was thought to jeopardize the Social Security bill (Marmor 1973). In a response to an inequitable distribution of medical services, President Truman, in his Fair Deal legislation, took up the cause of government-sponsored health care. In 1949 three senators proposed a bill that would remove money barriers between illness and therapy and that would legislate equal "protection" against ill health. The Congress refused to hold hearings on the bill, however.

In the 81st Congress, a coalition of anti-Truman southern Democrats and Republicans succeeded in blocking most of the president's domestic proposals, causing an executive-legislative stalemate. But a narrower form of national health insurance was worked out, which was to be limited to beneficiaries of Old Age and Survivors Insurance and would fall under the umbrella of the Social Security system. This plan set the stage for future Medicare proposals.

In 1958 in the Eisenhower administration, the Forand Bill was introduced, followed by the Kerr-Mills proposal of 1960, a bill supposedly attractive to conservatives because it restricted aid to those in severe financial need. The King-Anderson proposal of 1961 followed, which proposed an extension of Social Security benefits to cover hospital and nursing home costs, but provided for no surgical benefits. The Social Security tax was to have been increased to pay for coverage. The bill lacked bipartisan support from the powerful House Ways and Means Committee, which failed to take a formal vote on the measure.

During Lyndon Johnson's administration (1963–69), with his victory over Barry Goldwater being viewed as a win for Medicare, measures were taken to prevent any further holdups on national health insurance plans. At this time as well, the composition of the House Ways and Means Committee changed in partisan representation from 15 to 17 Democrats and from 10 to 8 Republicans. This meant relatively clear sailing for the King-Anderson bill which was introduced in January of 1965. The proposal represented only a beginning for national health insurance coverage (Marmor 1973). It provided for medical coverage of the aged, limited hospital and nursing home insurance benefits, and was financed through the Social Security system. The final proposal came out in July, 1965; the plan has been in effect since July, 1966.[3]

ANOTHER ELDERCARE OPTION

Adult day care is a rapidly growing option for the elderly, and political support for this mode is increasing each year (Weissert et al. 1989). Care in these centers, at least in the social-service-oriented center, is less costly than home care by a nurse and homemaker services and is more socially satisfying.

One of the minimum services that adult day care centers provide is social connectedness and interaction. Social connectedness is especially important in old age, according to social systems theory. Broadly speaking, the theory holds that if one's social connections are intact, satisfying, and of quality, most other facets of life are perceived as satisfactory (e.g., living arrangements).[4]

Many oldsters have only their social connections left to them; frequently they have "lost" financial security, family and spouse, mobility, good health, and agreeable housing. Having lost almost everything else, these social connections must be of good quality and, of course, must exist in the first place in order for the person to perceive life as satisfactory.

Speaking to the issue of social connectedness of the elderly is the move toward noninstitutionalization. This move is another healthy trend taking place in the United States. It has long been assumed that long-term care means care in an institutional setting. Thus there has been a proliferation of nursing home use in an abundance of cases where institutionalization has been inappropriate. In one instance, Barney (1977) determined in her two Detroit area studies that 40 percent of those in nursing home facilities could perform regular activities of daily living without assistance.

The elderly must have the prerogative of choice for their long-term care, according to Barney. Her study showed that there is a strong determination on the part of elderly people to maintain independent living, and therefore it is up to policymakers to place within reach of these elderly the types of services that promote self-reliance. Such services might be like those offered by the Well-Being Service for Aging in Detroit. This "storefront" operation offers transportation, ombudsman, counseling, homemaker, shopping, and health guidance, and social integration services in an "easy-on, easy-off" atmosphere. By that is meant that the elderly person finds it easy to physically and emotionally get in touch with the proper service and can move from getting information from one service to another as easily as one can move from "one chair in the living room to another." Services that promote this kind of independent living for the elderly need to be taken into account when employees are looking for ways to ease their dependent caregiving responsibilities. This service could be one option offered by an employer in a flexible spending account plan, as a good alternative to institutionalization.[5]

Not only will the care of the elderly in terms of their long-term needs be a future concern, but the quality of life of our chldren will increasingly be part of the public agenda. An investment in children now means that they will be better able to compete on our behalf later on (Allen 1989). And this investment is Allen's concern and focus of his article. We are "freeze-framed" in the 1950s, for the most part, maintains Allen, because we traditionally tend to consider family issues as personal-only concerns, and something to be left at the door when one enters the workplace.

HISTORY OF FAMILY, PARENTAL, AND DISABILITY LEAVE LEGISLATION

Family concerns as part of the political agenda were originally addressed in Title VII of the 1964 Civil Rights Act. Measures of familiy assistance particularized these concerns as "women's issues" and sprang from Title VII only in the form of the Pregnancy Discrimination Act of 1978, a bill mandating "even-handedness" in administering benefits.[6] On the state level, there followed an amendment to the Fair Employment and Housing Act in California. Although challenged as discriminatory to men, this amendment entitled women workers in the state government to an unpaid, four-month pregnancy leave with a job guarantee upon return. The challenge came from the California Federal Savings and Loan in August of 1983, charging that the amendment made women more "special" members of the workforce than men, subject to preferential treatment, and therefore the amendment was not compatible with Title VII. The amendment was held to be at odds with the practice of equal treatment of women and men workers (Radigan 1988).

This California challenge in turn was supported by Representative Howard Berman (D-CA) who drafted federal legislation that would make the measure national policy. Feminists, however, although somewhat divided on the issue, came up with a means to provide maternity leave at the same time ensuring equal treatment in employment benefits. That means, which would not set women apart as "special" and therefore tending to attract discriminatory treatment (e.g., occupational segregation and lower wages), was to extend job protection to all those who were "temporarily disabled." The temporary disablement clause included new fathers who wanted leave to stay home with their newborns. Women's concerns became men's concerns with this measure, and thus family concerns, and any measure giving attention to any one concern was to the benefit of the entire family.

To take maternity leave out of the feminist realm and put it into the family realm was to take it out of the feminist-liberal camp and put it into the pro-family/conservative camp, or, if not there, at least into the wider context of the centrist's camp. Fathers' as well as mothers' roles in nurturing the family now were being addressed; parental rather than maternity leave became the by-word. These concepts became known as the "equal treatment" approach to parental leave-taking.

As first envisioned by the drafting committee, a leave proposal was not to exempt any employer from providing parental and disability leave, and covered all employees with a disabling medical condition and those who needed to be home to care for a very sick child. The underlying principle was the entitlement of the right to leave-take in special circumstances with job reinstatement guaranteed. The proposal called upon employers to continue pre-existing health insurance benefits during leave.

The committee adopted a coalition-building strategy that included in its decision-making process and policy formulation such groups as the American Association of University Women, the UAW, the Service Employees International Union, and the Pension Rights Center (Radigan 1988).

When the committee submitted its bill outline to Congress, committee members were told it was "much too broad to attract attention." The universality of the committee's approach would be unacceptable to Congress, members were told. Representative Berman had already sent his own version of a bill to the House legislative counsel office (a staff of experts who put bill proposals into "proper" bill form); the bill contained his version of a parental/maternity leave idea. However, as time went on, Berman informed the committee that, although he could not act as their proposal's chief sponsor, he would not act against their interests either. In time, the concept of parental/disability leave was attributed to Representative Berman.

Bill H.R. 2020 was introduced in the House on April 4, 1985, by Patricia Schroeder (D-CO). Because several prominent Republican legislators had cosponsored the bill, it was considered somewhat bipartisan. The central theme was the bill's parental leave component. Its newsworthiness stemmed from the action of a U.S. court of appeals, which reversed the California district court ruling on the California Federal Savings and Loan case to acknowledge the Pregnancy Discrimination Act as compatible with Title VII. Further newsworthiness was gleaned from California Federal's appeal of the ruling to the Supreme Court.

At the time that Schroeder introduced the bill, she was senior woman in the House, chair of a subcommittee with jurisdiction over legislation providing parental and disability leave for government employees and cochair of the Congressional Caucus for Women's Issues. The committee found in Schroeder an ally, and Schroeder found in the committee's proposal an opportunity to increase an interest in women's rights and to broaden the appeal of a women's initiative.

A final proposal, introduced as the Parental and Disability Leave Act, included four months of unpaid parental leave upon the birth, adoption, or serious illness of a child, and six months of unpaid short-term disability leave, and provided for job reinstatement in both cases. Continuance and maintenance of pre-existing health insurance and other pre-existing employee benefits were provided. Employers who did not comply could be cited in a civil court action. A watch-dog commission was established to make recommendations based on a study of parental and disability leave-taking within two years of enactment of the policy. The mandate was to apply to all employers involved in interstate commerce and to all governmental entities at all levels.

Support for the bill was not unqualified, however. Labor groups found reasons to question certain passages, which seemed to threaten the seniority system. Disabled rights groups took the bill's definition of "disabled" to mean the total inability to perform a job, the notion of "total inability" being one that had been rejected as being negatively value-loaded by disabled rights groups for years. A revised bill was called for.

A larger, more diverse coalition was formed, with the additions of such groups as the AFL-CIO, the League of Women Voters, the Disability Rights Education and Defense Fund, and the Older Women's League. Redrafting ran smoothly for the most part. H.R. 2020 meshed well with existing labor law with regard to the seniority system, for example, and the redrafting took this into account. Disability leave was redefined as "medical leave," a more inclusive term, to satisfy disability rights advocates. To be exempted from the mandate were businesses employing fewer than five workers, making the bill more agreeable to small firms.

By the fall of 1985, the issue of parental leave was "ready for a national forum" (Radigan 1988: 19). A joint congressional oversight hearing was called for, which would determine leave policies among American businesses and therefore the federal response to the leave issue. The hearings generated no serious opposition to the proposal, and the new proposal was left intact.

Subsequently, early in 1986 a new bill, now called the Parental and Medical Leave Act, was introduced in March as H. R. 4300 in the House and introduced in April as S. 2278 in the Senate. Opposition was organized by the U.S. Chamber of Commerce, which saw the bill's specifics as a means for government to interfere in business, the bill itself as unnecessary since many employers had adopted leave practices voluntarily, as being discriminatory to women since its provisions would make the hiring of them unattractive to employers, and as forcing employers to sacrifice already existing benefits in order to provide the mandated ones. The opposition managed to shift sympathies of once-in-favor-of legislators as well as administrators toward the oppostion, the cost to employers of the proposed mandate of parental leave being the thrust of the shift.

A compromise was called for. It came in the form of raising the ceiling on the business size that the bill applied to, from 5 to 15 employees, on the length of allowed leave time to 30 weeks within a 12-month period, and the allowing of leaves to care for both the ill elderly and children. Time had run out for the 99th Congress, however, and the Legislation and Labor Committee, in June, 1986, had been bogged down by later committee maneuvers and debate. The bill could not be brought to the House before adjournment.

With the Democrats in control of both the 100th congressional House and Senate, the Family and Medical Leave Act (H.R. 925 and S. 249) was put at the top of the agenda. Family leave as a minimum labor standard and as ameliorating to families' basic struggles were themes encapsulated in proponents' arguments. Bicameral action took place almost simultaneously while the issue of cost to businesses was referred to the Government Accounting Office.

Skepticism arose in the House about the amount of "sympathy" that the bill's supporters had for small businesses as well as the bill's chances for passage. The balance between the needs of employers and employees and the length of allowable leave time under the bill's provisions were other concerns. Based on this skepticism, a subsequent compromise adjusted the size of employer to be covered to 50 for the first 3 years after enactment and 35 thereafter, and entitled employees to 10 weeks of family leave over a 2-year period and 15 weeks of medical leave during a year's time. It exempted short-term (less than a year) employees and those working less than 20 hours a week.

Allowance was made for employees who proved financial hardship to the company as a result of the policy and to deny leave to top salary earners. This compromise passed the House Education and Labor Committee in late 1987 (early in 1988 the House Post Office and Civil Service Committee approved of that section of the bill covering federal employees). At this point, the bill had 150 cosponsors and the endorsement of 70 organizations.

H.R. 925 was to have guaranteed job security for workers who took work-leave to care for a newborn, newly adopted, or seriously ill child. Under the act, seniority and health benefits were to be guaranteed for workers who took leave to recover from a serious medical condition. It called for employers of 50 or more for the first 3 years after enactment and 35 thereafter, to provide unpaid family leave of up to 10 weeks over a 24-month period upon the birth or adoption of a child or serious illness of a child or parent. Further specifications called for employers to provide unpaid medical leave of up to 15 weeks over a 1-year period in the event of serious illness of an employee. To qualify, an employee must have worked for the same company at least 20 hours a week for 1 year. . Reasonable notice of leave-taking was to be required. Employees in the top 10 percent of a firm's salary range were to be exempted if an employer could show business "necessity."

The Senate version of the bill, called the Parental and Temporary Medical Leave Act, proposed in 1988, would have exempted employers with fewer than 20 employees from the legislation. An employee would have been allowed to take up to 10 weeks of unpaid parental leave in circumstances specified in H.R. 925. The "reasonable notice" clause also was included. Employees would have been allowed to take up to 13 weeks of unpaid medical leave over a 12-month period when the employee was unable to perform the job because of illness.

As of September 1988, there were over 180 groups supporting family and medical leave legislation, including such groups as education, civil, disability, and children's and women's rights organizations, and labor, medical, senior citizen, and religious groups. State and local government groups also supported the legislation.

Job assurance in the face of meeting family obligations and needs was at the heart of this legislation. Giving employees the security of knowing that in times of great family need they can leave their jobs, speaks to the heart of the work-family conflict. The legislation would have provided families with essential options to meet concerns and responsibilities. More flexible work options for working families could begin to bridge the gap between home and work, and this was the rationale behind the legislation. This bill would have provided an allowance for workers to take leave to care for the elderly dependent parent as well.[7]

Another rationale underlying the bill was that family policies and the benefits of these policies were becoming increasingly important to workers when they evaluated employment opportunities and to employers who competed for working parents in the labor market. Proponents commended all of the bill's sponsors for focusing public attention on the relationship between employees' personal and employment responsibilities.

Both versions of the bill appeared to be partisan in that, with very few exceptions, all cosponsors, as of September 1988, were Democrats. Only 12 percent of the cosponsors both in the House and the Senate were Republicans.

Introduced in the 101st Congress (1989), the Family and Medical Leave Act was sponsored by Senator Christopher Dodd (D-CT). It was scheduled for consideration March 8 in the House Education and Labor Committee. The Senate Labor and Human Resources Committee gave an 11-to-5 approval to the measure's $2.5 billion program of direct subsidies to working parents. The measure would provide benefits to families with children up to age 15 whose family income does not exceed the median income of the state in which they live.

The House bill provides 15 weeks of unpaid medical leave in a 1-year period, and 10 weeks of unpaid family leave for birth, illness, or adoption of a child or for illness of a dependent parent over a 2-year period. The Senate bill mandates the same benefits, but only for those firms with 20 or more employees and those employees who had worked 900 or more hours in the past year. Under both bills, job reinstatement would be guaranteed and health coverage would be continued for the employee on leave.

How will the Family and Medical Leave Act fare in the 101st Congress? What is the chance that employers in private sector industries will be looking down the barrel of a mandated benefits program? Finegan (1989) gave parental leave and maternal leave only a better-than-average chance of passing. Although the long-term home health care proposal, the "pet" program of Senate Majority Leader George Mitchell of Maine, did not fare too well in the 100th Congress, it was predicted to do better in the new one. Patricia Schroeder reported that the Senate had taken up consideration of its bill only in the last two weeks of the legislative session and a Republican filibuster kept the issue from coming to a vote. The bill was pulled from any further consideration thereafter.

Again, opposition to the bills came mainly from business groups, and this opposition continues in the 101st Congress, according to Finegan (1989). Such opposition comes from such groups as the U.S. Chamber of Commerce, the National Association of Manufacturers, and, although small businesses would be exempt from the leave act, from the U.S. Chamber of Commerce on Small Business, concerning Section 89 of the IRS code, which is designed to eliminate employers' providing more attractive benefits to highly paid employees, citing costly compliance apparatuses and vague specifications of qualifications and compliances as devastating especially to small business.

Diamond (1989) reports that a House-Senate conference committee has agreed on a $1.2 billion bill to subsidize child care for low income families. The bill was to have been sent to President Bush before the Thanksgiving recess. Opposition to Dodd's (D-CT) bill came from Republican leaders who said it was just another layer of government interference, and Bush maintained that he preferred tax breaks for families rather than subsidies. The legislation would increase direct federal child care subsidies to low and moderate income families in 1990 by $1.2 billion and by up to $8.5 billion over the next five years. Under the bill, more money would go to rural areas at governors' discretion and states could issue vouchers that parents could use to pay for day care services provided by churches. Dodd sees the bill as a way for welfare mothers to work without having to abandon their children.

Small businesses especially continue to be concerned that the cost of family leave and child care policies will put an "undue burden" on them, and thus cause them to fail (Spalter-Roth and Willoughby 1988). Yet all businesses and taxpayers must pick up, in some way, the costs of public support programs in the absence of social policy. Lack of parental leave policies has been estimated to "cost" $715 million in income not earned by women who need to miss work because of childbearing.

If that part of human capital theory speaking to the relationship between income and GNP per capita is valid, then earnings lost translate into a loss in GNP per capita. According to this theory, human capital, as utilized in the market sector of the economy, "produces" earnings that become part of national income accounting. Lost earnings, then, are a loss to the national income level. National income level is the traditional and most objective indicator of a country's economic growth and a measure of a country's economic health. Economic growth, in turn, is one indicator of a country's economic development, development being indicated by a variety of social, political, economic, and demographic factors.

All workers in the market sector comprise our pool of human capital. A decrease in the supply of human capital, because human capital generates earnings, will amount to a decrease in national earnings. We have seen, though, that there is an increase in the labor force participation of women. According to Spalter-Roth and Willoughby (1988), this has amounted to employment growth, which, in turn, leads to economic expansion. Therefore, conclusions support the contention that labor policy promoting entry into the labor force and, most importantly, keeping those entrants steadily employed has positive effects on the economy. The intent of the Family and Medical Leave Act is to do just that.

PRIVATE INDUSTRY AND THE FUTURE OF
DEPENDENT CARE BENEFITS

Faced with a future labor shortage as children of the baby boomers reach working age—and there are far fewer of them than there are of their parents—companies will continue using ways to entice people into their labor pools, such as offering child care assistance. Few companies are untouched by child care difficulties faced by their workers, claims Wojahn (1988), adding that firms are convinced that child care assistance to employees, rather than being a fringe benefit "fad," is a good business practice because it pays off in terms of worker productivity.

Wojahn exposes some myths about company-sponsored child care services. To the first myth statement "We don't need it," Wojahn answers with the demographics of the size and composition of our labor force at the turn of the century (discussed in Chapter 1). Regarding the number of nonworking mothers with young children, she counteracts with the results of a 1982 Census Bureau survey, which revealed that 26 percent of these mothers would be in the labor force if reasonably priced and quality child care assistance were available.

To the second myth, "child-care assistance means an on-site center," Wojahn suggests alternatives used by some companies: information and referral services that direct parents to child care services, flexible work scheduling, and a voucher system. She cautions that a company should conduct a needs survey to determine what plan is most appropriate. "We can't afford it" and "we're too small and understaffed," other myths that may impede the motivation to provide child care assistance, may be true of on-site centers, but alternatives cost relatively little, especially after the first year of a program's operation. Even for small companies, such as the 24-employee Oliver Wight Company in Essex Junction, Vermont, which subsidizes 50 percent of the cost of operating its center for 11 children, the costs are not "outlandish."

A 1984 survey of companies found that 95 percent of the responding firms believed that the benefits of their child care assistance outweighed their costs. Thus the concern that "we don't get much back for all the expense and trouble" may be invalid (Wojahn 1988). Benefits may not be quantifiable, however, but are noticed in positive employee feedback, improvements in retention and recruitment, and a more dependable work-force. Add to this list the offering of child care assistance as good public relations. With regard to liability costs, companies are able to buy liability insurance for operation of on-site centers at a fairly reasonable cost—premiums run about fifty dollars a year per child, according to a spokesman for an Austin, Texas, center. There has been no known "successful" liability case against any business-sponsored child care center to date. Liability exposure is not a big risk for these companies.

The fastest-growing child care assistance plan for working parents is company-sponsored. This would be especially attractive to low income earners, infers Fierman (1988), who states that only 3 percent of the poorest 30 percent of the nation's families benefit from the dependent care tax benefit and they make up the workers who generally cannot take advantage of employee benefits packages such as flexible spending accounts.

Over four hundred company-sponsored child care programs, the number known to exist in the early 1980s, were studied to determine perceived and documented effects of the existence of these programs. Reduction in employee turnover, tardiness, and absenteeism, improved productivity, and increased recruitment, especially of secretarial, computer program, high technology, and assembly workers were reported. Of the 179 firms responding to a survey, none reported negative effects. Programs seem to be appropriate for large (more than five thousand workers) as well as small (fewer than one hundred workers) companies, with larger companies tending toward the provision of on- or near-site operations.

Of the employers with services, about half support care centers for children of all ages and some accept children of parents outside the company. A large proportion of these centers are affiliated with hospitals. Some offer supplemental services such as dental care, transportation, and counseling for both children and parents.

PIONEERING PROGRAMS

Other employer-supported child care services being initiated include voucher and subsidizing plans, referral and information support through contributions, in-kind donations, grants for community child care programs, parenting skills education, and other support programs. Polaroid, with its pioneering voucher program, pays up to 80 percent of an employee's child care bill if the family's annual household income is less than $30,000. Subsidizing day care homes through a coalition has been the focus of Bank America's California Child Care Initiative. Johnson and Johnson recently announced a broad work-family initiative that includes support for childcare and eldercare (Rodgers and Rodgers 1989).

Emergency child care plans for employees are a relatively recent innovation being adopted by some companies. This type of plan is an answer to the dilemma faced by working parents when not having someone to care for a sick child means that one parent must miss work. When emergencies arise, balancing work and family responsibilities becomes especially difficult.

Con Edison of New York City, discussed earlier, has such a pilot program.[8] The program covers those with children who are mildly ill, that is, recuperating from an illness, and who have not had a temperature above 102 degrees Fahrenheit for the preceding 24 hours. The illness must have been diagnosed by a physician before the child care service can be provided through the plan, in the case of children age one or older. The plan also covers the contingency of when the usual child care arrangement—school, day care center, care provider—cannot or does not work out. The program may also be used when an unexpected business trip was to be made and when an employee's work schedule changes unexpectedly.

Use of this program is limited to 3 consecutive days at a time, for a minimum of 4 hours a day and a maximum of 10 hours a day except in special circumstances. Certified caregivers from Selfhelp Community Services, Inc. in New York City and Contemporary Home Care Services provide the service. Both agencies are certified as health care providers and both have client-referral contracts with local hospitals and city agencies. Both maintain 24-hour telephone coverage. Both provide caregivers on a "best effort" basis at least, but every effort is made to provide certified caregivers.

Selfhelp's rate for up to 12 consecutive hours of service in a 24-hour period was $10.80 an hour from January 1 to July 31, 1990. Daily rates of $172.80 from January 1 to July 31, 1990 were charged for an employee using 12 or more consecutive hours of a service in a 24-hour period. Selfhelp's rates do not increase if care is provided for two or more children or on major holidays.

Contemporary Home Care Services, operating for those living in northern New Jersey, charges hourly rates of $10.50 for care for one child and $11 for two or more children. These rates also apply to employees using more than 10 consecutive hours of service in a 24-hour period. On major holidays, Contemporary charges hourly rates of $15.75 for care for one child and $16.50 for the care of two or more children.

Con Edison pays 90 percent of the cost of the program for the first 10 hours provided during the pilot period and 75 percent of the cost of any additional hours of service. The 10 percent and 25 percent that employees must pay are in the form of a payroll deduction, and amounts are deducted from the paycheck in one lump sum during a calendar month.

Federal income tax implications of using the plan depend in part on whether the employee has a dependent-care reimbursement account under the company's flexible reimbursement account plan for management employees. An employee with this account may be reimbursed (if a reimbursement request form is filed) for emergency child care payments with before-tax dollars. Under the present law, the emergency child care plan payments for services provided are not taxable income reported on an employee's year-end W-2 form. The present law states, however, that an employee may not receive more than five thousand dollars in a calendar year in tax-favored benefits from an employer-sponsored dependent care assistance plan. This means that for an employee with a dependent care reimbursement account and the emergency child care plan and who allocates the five thousand dollars to the dependent care reimbursement account, benefits received under the child care emergency plan will be additional taxable income reported on the year-end W-2 form. In any case, any amount of benefits received under any plan or combination of plans over five thousand dollars will be considered additional taxable income.

The insurance industry is taking some steps in the direction of helping employers help employees with dependent care responsibilities. Lewin and Wallack (1989) identify a new employee benefit being offered by a limited number of companies. Aetna Life & Casualty, the Travelers Companies, and John Hancock financial services offer to employers of 10,000 or more, nursing home, home health care, and adult day care coverage for their workers. Proctor and Gamble and American Express also offer similar coverage.

PROSPECTS FOR UNION INVOLVEMENT

UAW spokesperson and former president Douglas Fraser sees more cooperation between labor unions and management with regard to dependent care in the future, and Joyce Miller, president of the Coalition of Labor Union Women, sees unions as viewing work-family issues from the perspective of both men and women. Moreover, day care provision and dependent care assistance are becoming more of a part of union negotiations and leave policies. Certain union groups have found that a high proportion of members would like assistance in identifying care providers, for example. Union activity on behalf of workers' dependent care needs includes the establishment of a day care center financed by both employees and management by the Amalgamated Clothing and Textile Workers Union in 1968. The American Federation of Government Employees at a 1984 convention decided on a union-sponsored, community-based day care center as a pilot program. Other union activity on behalf of the work-family dilemma has taken the form of the adoption of a "Work and Family" resolution in 1986 by the AFL-CIO's executive council. The resolution urged affiliates to seek family strengthening programs through collective bargaining, programs such as day care centers, information and referral services, flexible hours, and time-off allowances for child care (Bureau of National Affairs 1986). Committees of labor and management have been set up in other businesses to address alternative work scheduling, the child care issue, and parental leave arrangements. In 1983, Local

8-149 of the Oil, Chemical, and Atomic Workers held a conference for its members. Finding a need to address work-family issues, the local was to set up a work-family committee at each work site.

Employees at AT&T can look forward to a rather comprehensive dependent care package. In May, 1989, just before a contract expired for about 160,000 industrial workers, the Communications Workers of America union and the International Brotherhood of Electrical Workers negotiated a three-year "innovative" package of family benefits (*Gazette Telegraph* May 29, 1989). The package allows leave-taking for as much as a year to care for sick dependents, payment of certain adoption expenses, flextime to attend to family emergencies, as well as a five-million-dollar child care fund. This fund will be supported by AT&T; it will be administered to support new and existing child care centers. Employees can use this tax-deferred account to save up to $5,000 a year for child care or eldercare. This agreement is the first of its kind on the national level, according to a spokesperson, and reflects the growing "power" of families in the work-force because the most significant provisions in the agreement deal with family care assistance.

With a decline in traditional industrial union membership and a shrink-ing labor pool, attracting people to jobs by making jobs more appealing is becoming increasingly important. This contract and incumbent negotia-tions leading up to it are seen as precedential for other industries seeking to attract workers. It is precedential because of AT&T's known leadership position in the communications industry.

Allen (1989) speaks to what the contract negotiations between AT&T and its unions have amounted to in terms of providing for our children's future, at least the future of AT&T employees' children. The company is putting money and time into building a network that links interrelated programs offered in schools and the community, one having to do with career counseling. (Three programs are being funded this year; six more will be funded within the year.) The necessity for having such a program lies in the fact that by the end of the century, four out of five jobs will require more than a high school education. Only those with more than that level of learning will be able to compete for the better paying jobs in the higher status occupational groupings (e.g., the professions). The type of training of our workforce ensuing from career counseling will allow the United States to join the world's leaders in business, according to Allen.

Yet, in spite of all the activity by government and private industry on behalf of the family, resistance to accommodating workers with dependent care responsibilities still persists. Sandroff (1989) maintains that the general failure to accommodate the family needs of two-career couples who have flooded the workforce is based on the mistaken perception that child care is a women's issue; that women workers who lobby for maternity leave and flexible hours do not have the company's finances in mind. This perception, however, is beginning to dissipate in light not only of the number of women entering the labor force, but the realization that it is not only women but men as well who are increasingly affected by family policies. Thus in order to keep the family afloat financially, it is in the best interests of men whose wives work to make a vested interest in making it possible for their wives to keep their jobs, no matter what the wives' salaries amount to.

Being on the "parent track," rather than the "mommy track" is becoming more appropriate to describe both men and women workers' roles vis-à-vis job and home. Being on the parent track means that employers must realize that both sexes need and want work flexibility to be able to accommodate home factors. Parent tracking as an entitlement is becoming more "attractive." Nearly 8 of 10 women as well as men prefer a job that gives them adequate time for their families even if it means slower career advancement; two-thirds of 1,000 male and female workers surveyed would be willing to reduce work hours and salaries to gain more free time with their families (Sandroff 1989). At the DuPont Company, it was discovered that half the women and a quarter of the men who use child care have considered changing to a job where the employer offers flexible work arrangements. But sometimes all it takes to accommodate family needs is a minor alteration in work scheduling such as permission to cut back to a four-day week for a while, a change to a position that does not require traveling, or to assignments that can be handled from home in case of emergency.

SUMMARY

Evidence suggests that there are activities and trends in both the public and private sectors that direct attention toward the family assistance needs of workers. "Parental leave" is taking the place of "maternity leave," although men still appear to be cautious about what is called parental leave. Yet, men are taking a greater role in child-raising and its incumbent issues, partially because so many of them are becoming single parents.

Dependent care assistance is receiving wide media coverage and considered to be the issue of the day, what with the increasing concern over affordable and safe dependent care facilities and the number of people in need of them. There is an increasing merger of private and public interests on this issue as well. States, for example, are beginning to offer more incentives in the form of tax credits to companies to shore up their dependent care assistance plans. According to Trost (1989), 13 states provide such a credit for child care assistance and 21 others have had bills pending in 1989 legislative sessions. Some states require employers to provide a disability plan of their own or subscribe to a state-sponsored one. Several provide state funding for such needs as affordable child care, child care for children or those participating in job training programs, and to increase day care licensing capacities.

Child care support legislation is relatively new; it was first formally introduced by the Lantham Act of 1942 during World War II when so many women were in the labor force taking the places of men in service. Not much happened with regard to child care legislation until the 1970s. Although some reductions in past measures took place in the early 1980s, the late 1980s saw a flurry of child care and parental assistance activity.

The Older Americans Act of 1965 set the stage for a number of eldercare provisions, including Medicare and Medicaid, the creation of area agencies on aging and adult day care centers, and community services to prevent the elderly from having to be institutionalized.

Title VII of the 1964 Civil Rights Act set the scene for what is now being called parental leave. Title VII was largely a mandate speaking to equality in employment. Philosophical issues arose from it as did problems with defining who was eligible for help under this measure. The job-reinstatement guarantee issue was problematic as well. Representatives Howard Berman (D-CA) and Patricia Schroeder (D-CO) were formulators and chief promoters of family and parental leave legislation in the mid-1980s. Typically, Chambers of Commerce and other conservative groups have opposed such legislation.

Proponents of this type of legislation point to the cost to the public of not having federal and state support for dependent care assistance. Income-not-earned because of being absent from work comprises part of this cost, which eventually becomes part of national income accounting.

Myths abound as to the need for and cost of child care assistance vis-à-vis the workplace. Wojahn (1988), however, explores these myths and finds them to be invalid. In most cases, for instance, the benefits of child care assistance outweigh its costs; the need for assistance is clearly there, too. Several companies are taking the initiative in this regard; pilot programs are underway. Unions, too, are initiating and supporting programs.

Finally, there is still resistance to dependent care assistance, resistance based on such notions that family responsibility needs pertain to women only and that a parent track for career advancement does not exist; only a mommy track does. But, increasingly, men are beginning to take a more active interest in child care issues and are wanting to become more involved in them. This increasing interest and involvement hold the potential for important changes in the ways employers perceive and act upon dependent care assistance.

NOTES

1. A spokesperson for a utilities company in New York State gave the rationale for the company's pretax allowance for child care as being that the government permits such an allowance under a 1981 law, making it possible for employers to provide child care benefits as a nontaxable compensation to employees.

2. But tax credit subsidies for low income families with child and dependent care expenses should be redressed, according to Fierman (1988), who suggests disallowing dependent care tax credits to those families with over $50,000 in earnings per year. More moderate tax credits had been proposed by the Bush administration as of March, 1989. For families making up to $13,000 a year, a $1,000 tax credit for each child under four would apply under the Bush proposal. If a family's tax liability is less than $1,000, a refund would reflect the difference between the amount owed and the $1,000 credit.

3. Medicare took on a "new look" in 1989 and added another dimension with catastrophic health care provision. Funding was to have come from all those over 65 years of age who would have paid an annual surtax of $22.50 per $150 of federal income tax liability, increasing to $42 per $150 of tax liability by 1993.

4. Other services possibly provided by adult day centers are case management, health assessment, nutrition education, therapeutic diets, transportation and medical services, and speech therapy.

5. Of the 617 cases handled in a nine-month period by the Well-Being Service, only nine had to be placed in an outside-the-home facility, most likely a nursing home.

6. The Pregnancy Discrimination Act is limited in ways. First, it applies to companies with 15 or more employees that already provide disability benefits; less than half of the country's employers offer disability benefits and only 40 percent of women work for these companies. Second, the PDA does not mandate job guarantee. Third, the act is not gender-neutral because it applies only to women.

7. Conservatives, who are often Republican, often see the enactment of child care legislation as undermining the family and leading to the "Sovietization" of child-rearing.

8. The pilot program runs from October 2, 1989, through July 31, 1990, and calls for a periodic evaluation.

6

An Agenda of Concerns

We have seen how both public and private industry is responding to the dependent care assistance issue on the behalf of employees and why dependent caretaking has become an issue in the first place. It now seems appropriate to set out an agenda of concerns that continue to be the subject of much media attention and bear watching because they are in such a dynamic state. The state of catastrophic health care for the elderly as embodied in Medicare legislation is a case in point. In mid-November of 1989, the House repealed the catastrophic health care provision from the Medicare program.

The nature of our response to the dependent care assistance issue is driven, in large measure, by the nature of our society's values. Salisbury (1982) discusses the various values held by society during certain decades and trends that affect the nature of worker benefits. During the 1950s, materialism, upward mobility, and "faith" in an expanding economic system were prominent values. In the 1960s, materialism drew people into a quest for self-actualization and self-fulfillment, a trend that has continued through the 1980s for the most part. This focus on fulfillment of self was the result of demographic and economic changes: baby boomers were well into the labor market and reaching the peak of their careers, and the growth in our elderly population meant that people were beginning to change their plans about the future. A new kind of economic realism emerged in the 1970s and 1980s—no longer was our economic system expanding. We could not expect the system to do for us what it had done in earlier times. These trends and others affected the nature of employee benefits. Along with the erosion of the egalitarian spirit and a greater acceptance of meritocracy, came greater support for a reduced government role in "private" affairs. Support for a reduced role of government led to more employers adopting more benefit programs for employees.

Accompanying the erosion of the egalitarian spirit came greater pluralism, flexibility in life-style and working life, and a greater sense of individualism. Blurring of sex roles will continue to make it easier for women to enter the labor force and go into careers. The 1980s saw an increase in the belief in the free enterprise system; we want our cooperations to do well. To simplify our lives, to reduce stress, and to create the personalization we seek so diligently, our "faith" in technology has been heightened.

All of these trends have tended to heighten our belief in individualism, which has tended to focus attention on human rights, problems, and individual worthiness. This belief in human worthiness has led to a realization that it is only from the human factor of production that all production emanates. Humanizing the labor process, mode of production, and the relations of production, then, makes good business sense. To do this, we must pay more attention to the social needs of workers. These needs relate to family matters, single-parenting, the way we treat the elderly, and the position of children in our society.

The family-in-crisis is a concern presently before the public, a concern that sometimes focuses on the economic suffering of children. The causes of this crisis are still being argued. Some say it is the result of the high divorce rate; others, that it is the result of women entering the labor force. In any event, there has been a restructuring of the family in recent years, but it is not *necessarily* this restructuring that has caused families to experience financial difficulties. Rather, it is structural factors—the destruction and displacement of highly paid blue collar employment, the dilemma imposed by welfare capitalism, and changes in job compensation—that go far to explain families' financial situations (Coontz 1989).

Coontz maintains that little can be done to solve the problem of family poverty by reviving traditional family structures. In fact, it is breaking with these traditional family patterns that has kept many families out of poverty. In the 1960s, 60 percent of the "bottom" category, in terms of family income, would have experienced an income loss had it not been for working wives. Coontz (1989) cites the University of Michigan's Panel Study of Income Dynamics, which has followed a representative sample of families since 1968. It found that only one-seventh of childhood transitions into long-term poverty were the result of family breakup.

Actually, changes in labor force participation and wage compensation were associated in over one-half of the cases with these transitions; a majority of the increase in family poverty in the past 10 years occurred in families with both spouses present. Forty percent of poor children live in two-parent homes. Labor force participation of men and job compensation, Coontz infers, explain to an extent why it is that in 1963 60 percent of men aged 20 to 24 earned enough to keep a family of three above the poverty level, whereas in 1984 only 42 percent managed to do so.

Education has to be factored into poverty statistics and taken into consideration when deciding what makes families poor. Between 1979 and 1986, the wages of people with a high school education or less declined by 17 percent, whereas for young men the numbers grew from 50 percent to 54 percent. The portion of men with a college degree decreased from 27 percent to 25 percent in this same time period.

Coontz questions whether changes in family composition and wives working are the root causes of the family crisis. It is, rather, job compensation including wages, salaries, vacation, and assistance benefits that need to be examined when we consider easing the crisis. Women are in the workforce to stay; men's rate of participation is declining. Families, whether two-parent or single-parent, as providers of labor for the market are an integral part of the work scene and should be accommodated as such. After all, "work and parenting are but two halves of a social whole: parenting is that process of creating mature and productive adults, who in turn through their work and service, contribute to society" (Bronfenbrenner 1988: 156). The following statement expresses this recognition of the importance of that accommodation: "What we would like our corporation to have is a work and family plan as part of its strategic plan for the corporation," so states a senior financial analyst with Manville Sales Corporation of Denver (Cotten 1989).

Societal values and perceptions about working mothers need some adjusting in light of this work-family conection. There are still many employers who see child care as a private family responsibility rather than a social one, and family responsibilities as the bailiwick of women only. Furthermore, arguments are made that shirking one's family responsibility because of outside work would result in delinquent, nonachieving children and marital discord leading to divorce. According to Nieva (1985), these arguments are largely unsupported and do not take into account whether or not outside employment is chosen or forced, the kinds and quality of child care arrangements made, the type of work done by mothers, and the husband's attitude toward his wife working.

Nieva argues for more consideration of the work-family linkage. Not only are expectations of role behavior changing, but the intervening variables between female employment and family factors need further discovery and examination. Among the questions begging for an answer are: Do family factors affect performance and turnover? If so, are the effects good or bad? What possible effects could a husband's support of his wife's working have on, say, productivity? What are the elements of a positive attitude on the job? Is there a linear relationship between work satisfaction and a satisfying family life? Do the separate roles reinforce or disrupt each other?

The positive aspects of enacting multiple roles—marital, parental, household—need investigation. The family-work relationship changes with the onset of various life stages (e.g., the "empty nest" situation) and factors such as the anticipation of retirement affect one's work. Interrupting one's career, experienced mostly by women, and then re-entering the workforce are topics that need examining especially in light of the usual high cost to train new workers to get them "up to speed." With the increase in the number of dual-income families, and thus more equality within the marriage, more men will be taking a break from formal employment or taking time to change to a more attractive career field. How career interruption affects men's career attachment and job performance will be a fertile field for research. Policies that support the maintenance of a functional relationship between the worker on leave and the organization might be formulated more clearly in the future.

A change in the way we look at paternal leave and part-time work is taking place. To some, the change heralds a change in sex role stereotypes; to others, paternal leave suggests "frivolity" (Lamb 1986). Even so, full-time work is still considered "masculine;" part-time is "feminine." Full-time equates with success, total dedication, and singleness of purpose. We find, therefore, that men will accept part-time and flextime work less frequently than will women. The same pattern emerges with regard to length of leave-taking: fathers take shorter leaves. Shorter leaves are considered less disruptive to a father's job prospects and career tracking. This change, then, needs to fit better with what is actually happening in the labor force with regard to men taking leave.

Employers' regard for part-time workers is a sensitive area needing examination. Although about 20 percent of our workforce is part-time, over 60 percent of these part-timers are women. Most firms, according to Sheinberg (1988), consider their part-timers as second-class workers. Gender discrimination in the workplace is hardly reduced by this view.[1]

Another suggestion for consideration on the part of employers vis-à-vis employee satisfaction and possibly job performance has to do with policies regarding re-entry after leave-taking and length of leave. The Catalyst (1986a) study revealed that parental leave-returners would prefer a period of three months after giving birth in order to integrate the dual role mother and worker. The tendency was to take as much leave as one could and still retain one's regular job. However, partial salary replacement and unpaid leave—a plan representing two possible components of leave—prevent some women from taking as much leave as is needed.

Another area of concern for future directions involves public awareness and acknowledgment of the growing number of single parents, especially men. No longer is the single-parenthood of fathers a rare social occurrence, according to Smith and Smith (1980), given the divorce and custody statistics. Single fathers need the same kinds of social and economic supports, in many cases, that single mothers need, and what is probably more important, fathers need to feel that availing themselves of these supports is appropriate.

Men have very little socialization to prepare them for the caregiver role. Even so, Smith and Smith (1980) have found that single fathers are quite capable of carrying out all the necessary tasks of homemaking and caregiving, and enacting these roles is not necessarily disruptive to one's work life. Nor does the single parent father role hinder the attainment of career goals. In another study reported by Lamb (1986), four-day workers (men) spent a great deal more time with their children than did five-day workers. There is the potential here for greater parental involvement with children when parents have compressed work week scheduling. How are fathers responding to the availability of dependent care plans? In interviews reported by Lamb, when flextime is available, fathers and mothers take advantage of it equally.

We need to degenderize dependent care assistance benefits policies so that men realize that they are entitled to take time off from work for no other reason than to provide emotional and physical support to their spouses and children. To make men feel comfortable about taking paternal/parental leave, companies should first find out about the need for such leave and then, as a matter of course, communicate the existence of paternal leave as extensively and with as much neutrality as maternal leave is communicated. As it stands now, many men wishing to take leave because of parental responsibilities do so under the rubric of vacation and/or personal time.

Making it more acceptable and easier for *fathers* to take parental leave has advantages for children's emotional health and academic achievement, Davidson (1990) infers. Although Davidson is referring to father-absence as a result of divorce, he cites evidence that indicates that one-parent children show lower achievement in school than do their two-parent classmates, and exhibit more antisocial behavior. Fathers, too, play an important role in preventing drug use.

Policies concerning parental leave have focused largely on the disability of the mother after childbirth, and thus have overlooked child care needs and leave-taking of fathers (Pleck 1988). Nondiscrimination-in-employment principles enable fathers to win leave benefits equal to those for mothers, however. What is needed, then, according to Pleck, is leave for purposes of providing child care. Parental leave rather than maternity leave is now the focus of legislation. Introduced in Congress in 1985 and 1986, and discussed at length in Chapter 5, such legislation would offer leave for both parents, with a job guarantee, *at least* on an unpaid basis. Under this provision, both parents could take leave for child care purposes.

According to a Catalyst study reported on by Sheinberg (1988), 37 percent of large firms extend an unpaid parental leave of one to six months with a job guarantee to men. But only a very few of the fathers working for these firms actually take the leaves. By not making parental leave a policy in-and-of-itself, the message is frequently that this type of leave may not be sanctioned by the company, and some workplace cultures simply are not conducive to men taking parental leave. Underuse of leave policies by fathers also can be attributed to the lack of clear communication about those leaves. In many cases, fathers, when searching for parental leave options, find them listed under such headings as "personal leave" or "emergency leave," for example (Catalyst 1986b: 131). New fathers may be unaware of how important their role might be at the time of the birth of a baby, so they reject the notion of leave-taking.

An issue to consider is how well fathers do in a nurturing role and how they perceive themselves in that role. Thompson (1986) reports that most studies of fathers in a caregiving role show that fathers felt competent, resourceful, and successful in their domestic responsibilities; most demonstrated the kind of nurturing and child-centered concern typical of most women in child care roles. In fact, most of the men in the study had not hired housekeepers or babysitters but had themselves assumed cooking, cleaning, and caregiving duties, and were "enjoying" them to an extent. Effects on the children of father-caregiving (in single-parent households) are also positive. For instance, there were no differences in emotional "atmosphere," self-concept, or self-esteem among children in maternal, paternal, or joint custody homes.

Lamb's (1986) thesis is that we are seeing a step in a series of changes in the conceptualization of a father's role in the family. Fathers are expected to be more actively involved in child-rearing, even though the effect of this involvement on children may differ according to circumstances. According to Lamb, over the last two centuries fatherhood as a role underwent four conceptual changes. During early times, the father was seen as a moral teacher and was endowed with the responsibility of bringing up children with an appropriate sense of values. Because moral values were based in the Bible, fathers educated their children to be literate so they could read the scriptures. Later on, with centralized industrialization (from the 1850s to the Depression), the father role was defined largely in terms of his economic contribution to the family—his role as breadwinner. After World War II, although moral leadership and bread-winning remained important functions, the father-as-role-model concept emerged to define the father's function in the family.[2] It was not until the 1970s that the notion of father as an active, nurturing, and caretaking parent arose, active parenting being the operative concept (Lamb 1986).[3]

Today's father often is deeply involved with his children on a day-to-day basis. The extent of involvement has been determined (although methodological and definitional problems in that determination are present). The three components of parental involvement generally are used for this actual time spent one-on-one, activities involving less intense degrees of interaction (the father sitting in one room while the child plays in the next), and the extent to which a parent takes final and ultimate responsibility for a child's care.[4] Fathers' involvement with their children has positive results for all concerned in the forms of cognitive development as the result of interacting with two people with different behavioral types, by allowing both parents a close relationship to their children while still pursuing careers, having good feelings about the domestic and marital states and about being at home.

COSTS OF ASSISTANCE

Salisbury (1982) predicts that the 1990s will be the decade in which firms will examine the cost of benefits programs and ways to keep costs under control. One way to do this is to get employees to shift benefits from the health area where cost increases are most likely to occur, to other areas like vacation and retirement, areas in which cost increases are slower. Wellness programs for employees will proliferate as a measure to minimize the use of medical benefits and reduce their costs. Direct cost awards and indirect incentives for not using benefits will be supported. Other emphases will be on home health care, ambulatory surgery, and pre- and post-admission testing.

Still lacking to a sufficient degree are adequate parental leave allowances and child care assistance. Approximately 67 percent of working women do not get maternity leave, and of those who do, they frequently are allowed only four months or less and with no pay. Of six million employers, only about four thousand offer any child care assistance, and if it is offered, employers usually provide only information and referral services.[5]

Of concern here also is the extent to which private sector businesses are willing to use tax breaks and such offered by states to provide child care services. Employer tax credits are a popular option among state legislators as a method to encourage employers to assist employees with child care (Trost 1989). Yet fewer than 1 percent of eligible employers use these credits: only one company in New Mexico has claimed the credit since it was established in 1983; in Connecticut, only .0005 percent of eligible companies were expected to claim the credit in 1989.

One of the reasons for such limited usage is that only businesses with corporate tax liabilities can claim credits and a smaller proportion of businesses have tax liabilities than have credits. In Michigan, for example, less than half of the state's businesses have any corporate tax liability. Then, too, tax credit programs are focused on start-up costs incurred with child care programs, but operating expenses may be greater than start-up costs. The administration of child care programs is often a concern of employers as well.

The New York-based Child Care Action Group suggests that states provide technical assistance to aid employers in implementing a child care benefit. Referrals to aid employers in understanding their child care assistance options and funding for a child care office within a state's economic development department are suggestions made by the Action Group to stimulate employers to develop child care assistance plans (Trost 1989).

The Catalyst report (1986a) cites poor communication of policy and inadequate information on existing policy as sources of policy underuse. Study participants reported that parental leave policies were "fragmented" between disability and personal leave policies. Communicating policy and programs can take several forms and they can be combined in a variety of ways, all discussed in earlier chapters. A clearly written policy, of course, forms the basis for supervisors and personnel officers to clearly communicate the policy. What supervisors and officers tell employees about policy must "match" perfectly with what is written. The way in which employees use the policies in practice must accurately reflect policy intent and directives. Where there is not perfect correspondence between intent and practice, employers should acknowledge policy flexibility unless they choose to see that employees follow policy directives to the letter.

The dependent care issue will continue to point up areas of concern that need addressing. One concern is the supply of good and affordable child day care, with the demand exceeding the supply two-to-one.[6] Families are hurting, claims T. Berry Brazelton (Nyborg-Andersen and O'Brien 1989), in an article in the *Ladies Home Journal*. With fewer than one-quarter of American families fitting the traditional family mode, we have a "national emergency." Finding quality care is of greatest concern. Most families seeking child care assistance must settle for a patchwork of services, a combination of care arrangements to include a relative, a neighbor, a limited-hours facility, a home care center, and/or an after-hours facility. The arrangements often generate stress and anxiety.

Day care that supports and strengthens the family as a whole entity must become the standard rather than the exception, according to Zigler and Frank (1988). To achieve this end, highly qualified staff need to be on board that appreciates and recognizes the importance of quality surrogating. To attract quality surrogates, salaries need to be increased. A survey of more than two hundred day care centers in Colorado revealed that teachers are quitting "in droves" every year because of salaries that average just over $8,000 a year. Teacher-directors earn an average of $5.83 an hour to start; directors earn $6.90 an hour. The highest average annual salary for teachers is $10,342 and for their assistants, $7,648.

The workload in many day-care centers is a problem. Staff members often have more work than they can effectively handle. Abuse by these possibly overworked, underpaid providers is reported. In March, 1989, a Chattanooga, Tennessee, sitter was sentenced to a year in jail after the parents of a six-year-old boy discovered she had been viciously slapping their child. A day care provider in Hartford, Connecticut, in August, 1989, was arrested after a three-year-old died in the woman's parked car, evidently from heat stroke. There have also been numerous incidences of charged sexual abuse.

Another problem with child care is its availability. Child care is hard to find, many care providers do not advertise, nor do their names appear on a master list. Even where lists exist, they are often out-of-date. Many lists do not indicate vacancy information, causing the seeker to spend much time on the telephone or on foot locating a caregiver. Infant care, wherein a high ratio of adults to children is considered desirable, is especially difficult to find. Before- and after-school care facilities are few and far between, as is care for the dependents of "off-hour" workers such as shift workers, police officers, and hospital employees.

In a study reported by Young and Zigler (1988), only 9 percent of nonprofit day care centers were described as providing superior care. There must be a standard for licensing and operating care facilities. Although all 50 states have regulations to guide the operation and licensing of day care centers, 44 states regulate family day care homes and only 14 states have specified regulations for group day care homes. State ratio regulations for infants in day care centers range from 1:3 to 1:8. In 16 states there are no ratio requirements for children under two; 18 states allow a 1:4 ratio for infant care (Young and Zigler 1988). The staff-to-child ratio for group day care set by the Federal Interagency Day Care Require- ments is not widely found in states. Clearly, regulations in this area are deficient. Zigler and Frank (1988) claim that caregivers themselves are inadequately trained and supervised.

In terms of staff training, there are deficiencies. Fifty-two percent of the states do not require the director of a day care center to have previous training in child care or development; only five states require operators of group day care homes to have taken a course in child development or care. In only eight states are caregivers required to have had training. In terms of quality and type of care in these centers, 58 percent of the states do not require developmental activities to be part of the care agenda. Even in states that did comply with this requirement, many of the centers indicated no method of putting into operation the mandated developmental program. Twenty states fail to specify any program of care for infants or toddlers in family day care homes. In many states there is no minimum age and/or education training requirement for a person to become a caregiver of children.

These deficiencies can be seen as the result of the withdrawal of federal leadership in standard setting, which has shifted the responsibility toward the state and personal levels, has caused the absence or lowering of state standards, and reduced funding.

State regulation does not guarantee quality care, however. In one instance reported by a working parent with a child care arrangement, the center took care of just the basics such as diaper changing. In another instance, when a parent visited the care center, the children were sitting passively in front of the TV set with a drum of popcorn on the floor in front of them. When asked what the children did when not watching TV, the parent's question was acknowledged by passive looks from the children (Nyborg-Andersen and O'Brien 1989).

Young and Ziegler (1988) recommend that state policymakers be allowed to benefit from the plethora of research findings on day care through a conference forum for policymakers, care providers, and parents. One piece of information to be dispensed during such a conference should be a cost analysis of quality day care (and the cost should not be prohibitive to low income families). Another outcome of a conference could be the establishment of a national day care clearinghouse for the use of legislators, providers, parents, and policymakers in all industries and the government. The conference format could serve as a training session for providers. Training of surrogates needs to address developmental problems experienced by children, parent-child relationships, the impact of the environment on children, peer relationships, cognition, and reducing stress caused by parent-child tension.

Then, too, parents need to be allowed to involve themselves in their childrens' outside-the-home care in the formation of a parent-provider partnership. Unlimited access to programs and periodic progress reports would be components of this partnership. Paid infant care leaves from three to six months for workers, both men and women, are recommended, which makes sense in the face of the disease-spreading that very young infants are prone to and for the strengthening of parenting skills so vital to the emotional health of infants.

Emergency day care services are another need for the future. In light of the relative costliness of hiring a temporary to fill in for an absent worker and the cost of missing work to deal with a child illness (the Child Care Action Group estimates the cost of the latter to be three billion dollars a year), some kind of temporary family help is called for. A consortium of New York firms began to experiment with this service in 1989. But this service is still in the experimental stage and needs further development.

Another direction that attention to dependent care assistance should take has to do with latchkey children. Even though some progress has been made in this area, out of the approximately 15,000 school districts in the country, only a few hundred offer some kind of after-school service for schoolchildren whose parents work. The effects of being at home alone after school are being studied; the general consensus seems to be that this situation can undermine a child's academic performance more than any factor (Nyborg-Anderson and O'Brien 1989).

THE FAMILY

Attention to the importance of the family and its concerns cannot be overemphasized. It is in the family setting that we become human. No group—church, school, day care—can replace the family, whatever that form may offer in terms of developmental conditioning. It is in the family that we learn to function well in other contexts; it is the family that should provide a loving environment to which we may "escape" when the "cold, cruel world" impinges upon us. It is the family that is the key nurturing force in our society.

But the family is not atomistic; it does not exist as an entity onto itself. It derives support—social, economic, and political—from society's other institutions. For example, businesses provide (or fail to) family benefits and job security to leave-takers, and the government mandates (or fails to) standards for day care provisions. Without this support, the family can become dysfunctional.

Yet, frequently this support steps in only after the family has proven inadequate in some way or other. We assume in our society that family integration and proper functioning will come naturally, that families can carry on somehow, can self-perpetuate simply because they exist. It is only after the family has shown that it cannot function adequately that remedial support steps in to "rescue." To qualify for support, the family frequently must document its inadequacy in a number of ways and show itself to be "inadequate" in categories recognized by support-givers. This mode of qualifying for support is called the Deficit Model by Bronfenbrenner (1988) and forms the base for the allocation of many public services.

Demographics and social trends have left the quality of family life in jeopardy. Working parents have little time for interaction with their children, parenting by fathers is given less time than parenting by mothers, mothers returning to work too soon after the birth of their babies can erode the foundation of the parent-child bond, and children are treated as objects by busy parents, to be dealt with in many cases in much the same fashion as dirty dishes and laundry.

Effects of these factors on children have been noted (Bronfenbrenner 1988). There is evidence that the family-work conflict reduces both the quality and quantity of interaction and is associated with lower achievement in school. Progressive deterioration in mother-child interaction following divorce and its disruptive effect on academic performance have been noted as well. Impaired well-being and development of children as a result of poor parenting, for whatever reasons, may contribute to rising rates of child homicide, suicide, teenage pregnancy, drug use, and juvenile delinquency, so infers Bronfenbrenner. Some of these effects have been shown to be associated with school violence and vandalism, becoming national patterns that are peculiar to all socioeconomic levels.

Citing Victor Fuchs' findings in *Women's Quest for Economic Equality* (Cambridge: Harvard University Press, 1988), Stone (1989) notes that there has been a general decline in the well-being of children in the last several years. This decline, it is suggested, can be blamed on the decline in parental care and supervision. Noting that we have barely begun to develop good child care or after-school programs or any of the other social supports that working families badly need, Fuchs argues for child-centered policies that reflect this concern, such as unrestricted grants to mothers of young children. Stone notes that, for most women, home is a "second shift," a shift that rarely lets up. And parents need to involve themselves more in this second shift, perhaps by firms having modified hours for parents of small children, and more flexible personal time provisions. "If a company's policies make it hard to respond when a child is sick or a day care arrangement falls apart or a parent conference is scheduled at school, balance between home and work will seem an impossible goal" (Stone 1989: 55).

Cutbacks in certain transfer payments such as Aid to Families with Dependent Children and competition with the elderly for funding from Medicaid, state and federal support for prenatal maternity care programs, Head Start, food stamps, and child nutrition and health programs are putting children, especially poor ones, at a disadvantage. If we are to maintain our standard of living and health in this country, more attention must be given to the needs of children. If not given by the public sector, the responsibility frequently falls to individual families. And in many cases, family resources simply are not there.

The financial situation of the generation known as the baby boomers is of great concern because, as Dychtwald and Flower (1989) maintain, baby boomers will eventually become caregivers of their own parents, a condition that will intensify around the year 2011 when the oldest baby boomers begin to retire. The question, then, becomes one of who will take care of the baby boomers at their retirement. They are not replacing themselves birth-wise and their real incomes are experiencing a relative decrease.[7]

Social Security will barely be available for the retiring baby boomers, according to Dychtwald and Flower, and only under the following unlikely circumstances: we have no recessions over the next 60 to 75 years, we have continual economic growth, the birth rate increases and longevity increases fewer than 5 years, and we do not dip into the Social Security savings pot. Since these condictions are "iffy" at best, baby boomers are well advised not to count on receiving their fair share of Social Security, but rather to save as much as they can on their own. Dipping into savings to fund dependent care works at cross purposes to this. "If the Social Security system continues as is, each working couple will, in addition to supporting themselves and their family, have to supply the entire Social Security income for one retired person throughout their working lives" (Dychtwald and Flower 1989: 68). This is an especially important statistic since, on average, people who reach 65 have about 16 more years to live.

What this all means is that the funds simply will not be there for the baby boomers to the extent that they are now there for current retirees. What this also means is that we must "take more" from our younger and middle years to finance our later ones. The burden of this imperative falls heavily on the working dependent caregiver if that caregiver is supporting a dependent with no outside help and especially if this dependent needs long-term care. Daniels (1988) estimates that about 80 percent of all long-term care is given by family members.

An increase in the size of our elderly population creates more dependency situations for middle age people than younger adults. The inadequacies of social programs such as Medicare and Medicaid, plus the tendency for the preference of home-based care, create a relatively large population of people who are being cared for by family members in the home. The family is still the major resource of its older members for emotional and social support, crisis intervention, and the link with bureaucracies. The tendency now is to get away from caring for the elderly in isolated, highly bureaucratized, and impersonal institutions. Still, the demands made by the elderly dependent may cause, in some cases, families to be shorn of resources and irrevocably damaged if there are no sustaining economic and service supports available outside the home.

A look at the dependency "burden" is in order. Lowering the retirement age increases the number of dependents who must be supported in one way or another. For each decade between 1980 and 2050, the increased number of workers retiring at age 62 will increase the number of dependents by 11 percent to 17 percent. Early retirement, now becoming the norm, has increased the financial burden on the present labor force. A continuing decline in the labor force participation of those over 65 years old is being predicted (Sheppard and Rix 1977). From 1955 to 1975, this participation declined at a rate of nearly 40 percent for those 65 to 69 years old. In 1956, Social Security benefits became available to women at the age of 62; for men, the year was 1961. This pre-65 retirement option appeared to be the impetus for other early retirement benefits to be offered by firms, some known as 30-year-and-out plans.

Early retirement is partly the result of employers' views of the "older worker"—that keeping an older worker is more expensive than hiring a younger one, that the older worker is less productive—as well as the demand for earlier and faster promotion on the part of younger workers. Reducing the workforce during times of economic recession may also encourage early retirement.

Increasing this dependency ratio is also the result of the increasing number of people who pursue a higher level of education. In the year 2000, it is estimated that between 51 and 62 percent of young people ages 18 to 21 may be enrolled in school; the percentage was 40 in 1970. A slower rate of getting out of a dependency status is indicated by these figures, meaning that "supporters" will be assuming a growing burden for dependents. Factored into this dependency burden must be the fact that many workers—teenagers, students, married women, for example—are economic dependents because they are part-time, low wage workers. The dependency burden is even greater if we consider supporters as being only those who work year-round and full-time.

Actual labor force participation projections give us a grim forecast of the dependency burden. In 1975 there were 123 nonworkers for every 100 workers; in 2010 there will be 103 nonworkers, an obvious decrease in the dependency ratio. But it is by the year 2010 that the baby boomers will begin to retire in great numbers, and there is a large cohort of them. After this time, then, unless there is a substantial increase in labor force entrants—unlikely because of decreasing fertility rates and baby "busters," the children of baby boomers, who will be parents by then and will have produced fewer children because there are fewer of them—we will see the dependency burden increasing.

THE ELDERLY

Concern over the U.S. elderly population is increasing as the number of elderly increases, especially those over 85 years old. There is concern over the shortcomings of assistance programs and the economic burdens imposed by our present health care system.

Many elderly have serious financial problems, and many of them have trouble coping with major medical bills. Weicher (1989) shows that between 1977 and 1983, low and moderate income households of elderly (with incomes under $8,500 and $8,500 to $17,000, respectively) with the household head age 75 and over suffered a decline in mean wealth ($36,300 to $22,500 and $73,200 to $71,800, respectively). Moderate income elderly between the ages of 65 and 69 also experienced a decline (from $64,000 to $61,500).

As current payment mechanisms for health costs increase and become more inadequate (the Medicaid program acts as an insurer of last resort, for example), and the very old live longer, there is greater need for assistance to help the elderly to remain in their own homes. The inadequacy of payment mechanisms creates financial risks for these people, especially those entering a nursing home in a long-term state of dependency. In a study by Branch et al. (1988) in Massachusetts, it was discovered that 46 percent of the single elderly 75 years and older would run the risk of spending down to impoverishment (at which time the person would be eligible for Medicaid) after only 13 weeks of nursing home care. Only one out of four would escape impoverishment in the first year following nursing home placement. Among couples, both of whom were 75 years of age or older, 25 percent of the households would become impoverished within 13 weeks, and one out of three of the younger elderly (66 years old) would become impoverished within the same period. These are rather startling figures given that, as of 1984, two in five Americans will spend at least some time in a nursing home before death.

Barney (1977) discovered from two studies of long-term care in Detroit that, of the 466 nursing home residents who had entered on a private-pay basis two or more years earlier, 259 of them were still alive but only 77 (29 percent) were still private patients. Moreover, many of those who were Medicaid recipients had been financially independent at the time the decision was made to enter a nursing home.

With the increase in the number of elderly aged 85 and over, a greater production of long-term services will be required. This age cohort will require over one-half of all long-term care services. For those 65 years and over, as it now stands, the problems with providing long-term care are multiple: Medicaid payments for the indigent are often insufficient, which means that a spouse or other family member must pick up the tab. There are few services, such as supplementary home services, to relieve caregivers. Care in institutions is not directed toward rehabilitation, although rehabilitation of the elderly person is possible in many cases. Frequently long-term care is not "medicalized" and, therefore, is seen as nonessential. Such "nonessentials" include cooking, shopping, bathing: the services most frequently needed by elderly dependents and considered necessary to compensate for and maintain "normal" functioning.

In light of less expensive alternative arrangements to nursing home care, the perceived overuse of nursing homes (Barney 1977; Brickner et al. 1976), and the impoverishing effects of institutionalization, the future holds other prospects for care of the elderly, prospects that will need social, political, and economic support for those providing care.[8]

Dunlop (1980) maintains that research on the assumed expanded benefits in the form of long-term health care services to the impaired elderly is inadequate, but allows that expanded home-based care for these elderly would reduce their institutionalization. Funding for home-based care outside of Medicare and Medicaid is needed because stringent financial eligibility criteria are imposed by states and this seriously restricts the accessibility of this type of service.

Dunlop asks questions about how many impaired dependent elders would avail themselves of expanded home health care services. How would the expansion of home-health services affect the rate of institutionalization? The message is clear. It is the family member caring for the impaired dependent who would ultimately benefit by expanded home health care services.[9]

Dunlop summarizes the utility of home-based health services. Their provision reduces the likelihood of institutionalization and allows gains in physical and/or mental competence on the part of the elderly person. Services have the potential for increasing contentment for all concerned, the reduction of tension between caregiver and receiver being critical. Dunlop warns, however, that there is a negative connotation to home health care services—they are considered welfare services. Therefore their use may be limited. Another limiting factor is the desire on the part of most elderly people to make it on their own.

With this orientation, finding alternatives to institutionalization are in order. Advocates for alternatives talk about the maintenance of autonomy, dignity, and self-respect for the dependent. Thus the importance of relatively independent living is underscored with the provision of home- or community-based services. But community services and facilities for long-term care, according to Meyer (1989), are in short supply and often inadequate and inefficient. Such conditions are often the result of "self-serving" licensure requirements that restrict the supply of services through limiting competition among health-care deliverers. Unnecessary licensure requirements limit the kinds of services that can be delivered by a health care provider. People who provide the services most frequently needed by elderly people—help with bathing, transportation to the doctor, and companionship—do not need a high level of education nor do caregivers need to be technically skilled; skilled providers, on the other hand, do not necessarily provide these services. Thus credentialism does not always serve well the needs of the elderly.

But federally sponsored programs to allow people over 70 to live independently have been dealt a blow. In July, 1989, Housing and Urban Development secretary, Jack Kemp, suspended a retirement service center program that provided mortgage insurance for housing developments for these people. (The program was intended for the low and moderate income elderly but had been fraught with mismanagement and abuse.)

The quality of long-term elderly care is being given much attention of late. It is increasingly becoming a "popular" cause taken up by gerontologists and health care professionals. Callahan and Wallack (1981) suggest improving the quality of long-term care. Their suggestions include using effective technical and organizational methods to motivate or control providers. But the implementation of these methods increases administrative costs and bureaucratic control over providers and, in turn, would not necessarily improve the quality of care. Something needs altering to properly and effectively provide this care, but Callahan and Wallack do not know the "right" approach, except to expand public expenditures, not a popular option.

Specialized funding geared to the type of cost to be met and by the site of delivery of services is suggested to improve long-term care quality. Cash payments and vouchers to individuals, although very costly, is yet another means. Local long-term care organizations could be established to assess, plan, coordinate, and control the flow of resources to direct providers.

Medicare and Medicaid fall short of adequate financial support to elders. Schick (1989) argues that we are spending more and protecting less with regard to such measures. In spite of Medicare and Medicaid, elderly people spend about the same percentage of their incomes on health services as they did *before* these programs went into effect. (The largest percentage of income spent on health care comes from the poorest of the poor elderly.) Cost controls and freezes on the price of medical services have done little to abate the inflation of service costs.

Medicare and Medicaid are "lopsided" and "unbalanced" says Meyer (1989). Medicare does not cover some of the health services most frequently needed by the elderly and fails to cover other costs as well. Meyer reports that budget and tax bills passed between 1980 and 1985 led to a 49 percent increase in payments for hospital, skilled nursing facility, and home care. In the same period, there was a 31 percent increase in out-of-pocket costs after Medicare's payment for physicians' services, lab fees, and outpatient hospital services. Most care paid for by Medicare is acute-oriented and given in an institutional setting, thus forcing some into choosing between institutionalization or receiving little or no care. Medicaid, too, is institutionally oriented.

Eakes and Landsman (1990) describe the changes in Medicaid effective September 30, 1989. Regarding the spouse who remains at home (as opposed to the one entering a nursing home), he or she may be entitled to a monthly maintenance needs allowance from the income of the spouse in the nursing home. This represents the amount required to raise the at-home spouse's total income to the basic income allowance, determined by federal law, of $815 per month. Federal law further limits the maximum monthly needs allowance plus shelter allowance (the amount of which his or her total housing costs exceed 30 percent of the basic income allowance) to $1,500 per month.

Assets belonging entirely to the at-home spouse are not totally protected, however. When one spouse enters a nursing home the local Medicaid agency will evaluate the couple's total assets to include all countable assets regardless of source or ownership. Excluded now are the couple's home as long as the spouse or a specified person lives in it, one car, a burial fund, and various other personal items. The at-home spouse is allowed to retain the greater of $12,000 or half the total assets to a maximum of $60,000; this amount can be increased by a hearing or court order.

Before qualifying for Medicaid, the spouse entering the nursing home must spend down to his or her share of assets to the resource limit of $2,000 to $2,500 (the amount determined state-by-state). Once eligibility is determined, assets held by the at-home spouse can no longer be used to determine Medicaid eligibility of the spouse in the nursing home. Five out of six elders cannot afford private insurance to cover nursing home care. Only 3.6 million of the 22 million Americans 65 years or older can afford it, the average cost at age 65 being $1,255 a year and, at 79, more than three times that amount.

Since the withdrawal of the catastrophic coverage law in 1989, Medicare will fully cover only the first 60 days of hospitalization after the patient pays a $592 deductible for each period of illness. The patient pays $148 per day in coinsurance for each spell of illness. Beneficiaries are liable to share costs of $296 per day for lifetime reserve days with the government (Eakes and Landsman, 1990). After these days are used up, the patient pays the entire bill.

A Medicare beneficiary must be hospitalized for at least three days before going into a skilled nursing facility. For each period of illness, Medicare will pay for all covered services for the first 20 days. For days 21–100, the beneficiary is required to pay $74 per day in coinsurance. After 100 days, the patient picks up the entire bill.

Medicare now covers up to 21 consecutive days for full-time skilled home health care of up to 35 hours per week for those who need skilled care less than four days per week. The beneficiary must be homebound and services must be ordered and reviewed regularly by a physician. Medicare now covers up to 210 days of hospice care. The program pays only for prescription drugs administered in the hospital and for immuno-suppressive drugs needed during the first year of an organ transplant. Respite care support has been withdrawn from the caregivers of beneficiaries, nor is payment for mammography screening now covered.

Limits to Medicare and Medicaid, as well the increasing need for more appropriate long-term care, clearly point to the need for development and use of alternative medical assistance plans such as supplemental insurance programs. But "Medigap," or supplemental, insurance, is generally beyond the financial reach of the poor and fails in other respects as well.[10] Lewin and Sullivan (1989) point out that this type of insurance is not readily available to those who need it, does not protect against financial catastrophe, and some providers will ask about existing health status, which limits coverage for pre-existing conditions. Requiring three days of hospitalization before the plan kicks in is another drawback. Getting people to buy this type of plan at an age when they can afford it instead of waiting until later in life when the policy is needed is another problem. This situation often comes about because people believe that Medicare and Medicaid offer comprehensive protection against long-term needs.

Other drawbacks to supplemental insurance are described by Lewin and Wallack (1989). State regulations may impede the development and provision of such policies; there is a question of what to charge for services; and the insurability of custodial services is problematic.

According to Moon and Smeeding (1989), the purchase of private supplemental insurance coverage could be encouraged by educating those facing retirement about what Medicare and Medigap policies actually do and do not provide, and about what the cost of long-term care is likely to be. Encouraging the elderly to liquidate their assets (for example, through home equity conversion) so that they can afford the premiums could be another option, as could subsidizing employers or employees who are near retirement so that they can buy long-term care insurance. Tax inducements could also be offered to both insurees and insurers.

Yet another eldercare element of concern and receiving attention is elder-abuse. Although most nursing homes, for example, seem to provide at least adequate care, horror stories about the abuse of residents abound (see Barrow and Smith 1983, Chapter 8). Nursing homes, however, are not the only offenders; families of the elderly, for a variety of reasons, often abuse their elderly relatives.

Elderly parents of children who are themselves besieged by financial, social, and psychological pressures, especially those caring for elderly who are frail and/or ill, are potentially at a high risk of being abused. "As the dependencies of the aged parent increases, both the aged and their adult children become more aware of potential conflict situations" (Barrow and Smith 1983: 113). The burden of an elderly person's physical, emotional, and financial support may be just too much for a caregiver to handle. Abuses of elderly persons at the hands of their caretakers involve financial, emotional, mental, social, and physical mistreatment. Any measures taken to reduce the stress level of a caregiver can reduce the likelihood of abuse. Physicians' reports of elder abuse helps to reduce this problem. Mandatory reporting on the part of physicians is required in some states, but there are weaknesses in the reporting requirements that may make reporting somewhat ineffective (Daniels et al. 1989).

WORKFORCE MOBILITY AND THE ELDERLY

Workers today no longer expect to stay in the same location throughout their working lives. As families are split geographically, the burden of handling family affairs often becomes more cumbersome and stress-producing. Long-distance eldercare and child care assistance from family members is less easily given than is short-distance care. One answer to this problem and a trend identified by Carlson (1989) includes services provided by mail-order companies specializing in products for the elderly, consulting firms that help employers recruit older workers, businesses that train aides for infirm older people, and national counseling networks that aid employees in dealing with long-distance eldercare.

Work/Family Directions in Watertown, Massachusetts, dispenses long-distance emergency advice when a parent of an employee faces a health crisis or the parent needs advice on living arrangements. This network service is being offered as an employee benefit in companies. Work/Family has its own contractors, mostly private, nonprofit agencies, in 150 locations across the country. Use of this counseling service is increasing and the concept is gaining in popularity. About 11,000 requests from IBM employees have been processed by Work/Family since February 1988. About 5 percent of the workforce at North Carolina National Bank can expect to call on eldercare counseling in a given year. The eldercare concept is included in the contract negotiated in the late 1980s between AT&T and its unions, and is on the bargaining agenda between Boeing Company and the Machinists Union. Aging Network Services, based in Bethesda, Maryland, is a counseling source representing individuals, law firms, and hospitals that uses a network of independent social workers to help the elderly through difficult times. The fee a company pays for an eldercare consultant ranges from $5 to $15 per worker, per year.

RISING COSTS-LIMITED SERVICE?

Who pays for dependent care costs of employees? It seems likely that employers are going to be less willing to absorb much of these costs in light of rising expenses of operating a business including costs of an employee assistance plan. A typical company medical plan, for instance, increased in cost by 20 percent to 25 percent in 1989, up from 15 percent to 20 percent for the previous year. Some companies have adopted measures to hold down these costs, such as negotiating for lower prices from certain dentists, doctors, and hospitals in return for a promise to send employees their way. Reviewing the use of certain services possibly to eliminate unnecessary tests and operations and to shorten the length of time spent in the hospital are other cost-reducing methods. Physicians who charge what is felt to be exorbitant prices are being challenged in court; some companies process and administer their own claims; others refuse to pay medical bills of employees who do not belong to a health maintenance organization; and some have set up their own medical clinics and pharmacies to reduce the health care bill. Others are shifting more of the cost burden to employees.

According to Daniels (1988), as we age, society's major institutions, especially the family, must adapt because aging causes changes in social needs—fewer children need education, more elderly need health care and income support, for example. We must redesign our institutions so that they accommodate social justice among the different age groups.

Another "justice issue" is quality versus quantity. Medical science keeps coming up with ways to keep us alive longer, but the quality of that longer life often gets the short end of the stick. We forestall death with life-extending resources, but we tend to overlook the urgent daily care needs of the elderly as they age. In a sense, then, the problems of our aging society are created by a successful medical technology and a social policy that has not kept pace. Institutions must also respond to the increase in the prevalence of chronic disease and disability, which "defines" our present age profile.

Since nearly all of us, at some point or other, will need care, comfort, and assistance from another human being, we all need to learn the skills that such caring demands. Bronfenbrenner (1988) suggests learning these skills from the earliest school grades onward by becoming responsible for spending time with and caring for the elderly, the young, the ill, and the lonely. Such learning would take place not only in schools, but in communities, care centers, and in neighborhoods. Another suggestion is to provide extension services in every community to create informal social networks, established through local initiatives and resources, to enhance parent empowerment through networking that links family members and provides access to needed resources.

Stoiber (1989) makes the point that family leave provisions should reflect a nation's values toward financial security, government intervention, leisure time, and equality. (In the United States, we are less security conscious than are Europeans, are far more geographically and occupationally mobile, and place a lower priority on leisure time than do Europeans.) Such provisions, when mandated, can be seen as political interventions in the labor market, and thus need to be judged according to a country's views of and values regarding such intervention. In the United States, although the political and economic sectors are interdependent, one sector should be "allowed" to function relatively independent of the other, and vice versa. Be that as it may, economic and political forces over the past several decades and for various reasons have caused an increasing merger of the two sectors.[11]

Our emphasis on minimum government intervention into private lives means that we have followed quite a different pattern of intervention than that established by countries of Western Europe. Fringe benefits such as parental leave have been established in these countries, making the integration of home and work lives less stressful. That is not the case in the United States.

One way in which our national ethic differs from that of other countries is that we have no strong sense of responsibility for other people's children. We have very little sense of "collective good" and a concern that whatever public actions are taken toward the care of children may undermine the "remaining capacity of the private family to provide for its children" (Preston 1984: 448). Therefore, we resist becoming dependent upon the state for we fear bureaucratic encroachment. We have adopted a meritocratic social philosophy; we believe that social benefits should accrue only to those who have earned them, and we value individual imagination and resolve. But the hazards of living—accidents, environment, environment-caused problems—are not distributed according to merit. Cancer and Alzheimer's disease know no social class bounds.

Easing the work-family strain will become a bottom line concern and a cause for involvement in dependent care problems of workers, according to Friedman (1986). Businesses are already feeling the results of this strain on workers and will continue to do so as more data on its effect on worker performance becomes available. Retention problems should ease as more companies expand their policies regarding working dependent caregivers. For example, Hewitt Associates allows employees who work late to be reimbursed for baby sitting expenses; the firm also plans to set up a child care center at a new facility. DuPont has lengthened its maternity leaves, allows more flexible work schedules, and has increased funding for a community child care center, changes made as a result of finding that 25 percent of its male and 50 percent of its female employees had considered looking for work in firms offering more flexibility.

A financial firm in a large midwestern city is looking to expand its present-day care provisions possibly to include everything from an on-site center to a referral service. Part of the expansion may include an arrangement for a corporate discount for employees' children at a local day care center. Adult day care centers are operating in Cambridge, Massachusetts, and in Scranton, Pennsylvania, to name just two of the more than 1,700 existing in the United States. Johnson and Johnson has beefed up its support for working mothers by introducing new support services, representing a revision in company policy, which had not been changed in 40 years. The firm is preparing an on-site child care center to be operating sometime in 1990 (Moskovitz and Townsend 1989).

There is wide availability of resources in the United States to address the dependent care assistance issue. One resource is the Catalyst group.

Catalyst, in New York City, continues to be innovative in their efforts on behalf of workforce issues. Catalyst, a national research and advisory organization, works with corporations to foster the career and leadership development of women, and aids senior management and human resource professionals to recruit and retain women at every organizational level. The group also serves as an objective, well-informed source for the media. It offers research and advisory services to include field research and research consortia, publications such as "How to Set Up A Plan When Your Employees Are Complaining," a speakers bureau, and an information center.[12]

In spite of all efforts by private and public entities, the dependent care responsibility situation as it impacts on those who work needs far more attention. Companies must create an environment in which employees with dependents can do their best work without harming their families' welfare. The communication of corporate policy pertaining to dependent care assistance is the first need. Next, companies need to train supervisors to be flexible and responsible, and they must have the proper "tools" with which to work. Finally, firms need to hold all managers and supervisors accountable for the flexibility and responsiveness of their particular departments (Rodgers and Rodgers 1989).

There must be consistency in what is communicated so that mixed signals are not sent down the line. First-line managers and supervisors must have a thorough understanding of policy and of the corporation's commitment to it in order to demonstrate a company's sensitivity to the work-family connection, as well as their own dedication to carrying out policy.

There are still many U.S. companies that give only lip service to the value of the family in a worker's life. These are the firms that must think about communicating to their employees that family issues are real, complex, and important, and cannot be separated from a worker's life on the job.

NOTES

1. Management's concern about part-time work and job-sharing, discovered by Catalyst researchers through a literature review and by conducting interviews with human resource professionals and over 150 other employees, include the beliefs that such arrangements will exceed benefits and therefore be costly, that it is impossible to perform a managerial- or professional-level job in fewer than 40 hours a week, that employees not in their offices full-time are less than committed to their careers and companies, and

that offering a flexible work schedule to some will create an across-the-board demand. Pertaining to these concerns, Catalyst found that only 14 percent of human resource professsionals cited cost as hindering implementation of a flexible arrangement policy; no one cited a heavy increase in demand for flextime as a result of implementing policy. To counter the perception that flextime was costly, a full-time equivalency system where two job-sharers count as one worker helps with this problem.

2. Their inadequacies in this regard were popularized through the media with such movies as *Rebel Without a Cause*.

3. The relative weight given each of these functions depends, of course, on the context in which these functions exist.

4. Findings from one study (Lamb 1986) reveal that from 1975 to 1981, there was an increase in direct interaction with children on the part of fathers, and this represented about a third of the involvement of mothers. Type of interaction varies by parent, too, mothers providing caretaking time and fathers providing "play" for the most part.

5. We have to keep in mind that it is usually (and naturally) larger firms that offer these kinds of services so that the four thousand who do may seem like a reasonable number even though a majority of people work for companies with fewer than 50 employees.

6. Expenses of child care facilities vary by area of the country, of course, but can vary from $2,000 to $10,000 a year, with infant care the highest priced. Sometimes these expenses can amount to about 10 percent of a middle class household's income but 25 percent of a poorer household's income. With the stipulation that parents must provide the names and Social Security numbers to the IRS to qualify for a child care tax credit, the cost of providers may be increased. The costs of child care frequently represent the second salary in a two-earner household. Then, too, costs of child care have risen dramatically with the increase in the demand for such care; the demand has created an underground cash economy of unregulated, non-reporting caregivers.

7. Younger workers need all the help they can get, then, and will continue to do so if poverty trends hold. The real income of younger workers has declined in the past several years as the economy went through recessions creating a poverty rate of 14 percent as compared to 12.4 percent for those older than 65 (in 1986). Nineteen percent of those between the ages of 22 and 64 lived below the poverty line in 1986.

8. For instance, home maintenance of the dependent elderly is about one-third as expensive as nursing home care.

9. Dunlop reoprts that in a high percentage of cases, primary support services deemed critical to the capability of providing elderly care in the home is provided by spouses, daughters, and friends. In one study of long-term needs of the elderly in New York City, only 15 percent of this care was provided by nurses, health aides, and home helpers. This trend is borne out by the fact that apparently those elderly having received sustaining care by a family member were admittted to nursing homes in a far more impaired state than those admitees without close kin.

10. More than 25 percent of elderly Medicare enrollees with incomes below $15,000, in 1984, had neither private insurance nor were Medicaid-eligible compared to 10 percent of those whose incomes exceeded $25,000 a year. Furthermore, the proportion of elderly without supplemental coverage rises with age and with poor health.

11. Sociologist C. Wright Mills, in his book *The Power Elite* (New York: Oxford University Press, 1959), maintains that there is a unified elite group in this country consisting of business-corporate leaders, government leaders, and top military personnel.

According to Mills' argument, whereas government sets some business "standards" thought to benefit the populace as a whole, business uses lobbyists in legislatures and makes contributions to campaigns and uses other techniques to influence the government process to their advantage. Many examples of this complementary relationship are given in Michael Parenti, *Democracy For the Few* (New York: St. Martin's, 1988).

12. Catalyst's address is Department M, 250 Park Avenue South, New York, New York 10003–1459. The telephone number is 212–777–8900.

Appendix A: The Questionnaire

February 1, 1989

As part of a book-writing project, I am trying to determine the extent
to which domestic firms are addressing the particular needs of workers
who are members of the "sandwich generation," that is, those who are
care-givers to members of both the older and younger generations.

As a recipient of questionnaires myself, I realize surveys are not
popular. With that in mind, I have devised a short survey which I am
sending to businesses throughout the country. The survey follows. I
am hopeful you will take the time to answer the few questions. You
may wish to use the enclosed, stamped, and self-addressed envelope for
your responses. If you desire to remain anonymous, please cut off the
top section of this letter.

I shall be grateful for your attention to my request and remain,

Cordially,

LouEllen Crawford
P.S. If you would like a copy of the results of the survey, please
     indicate this - YES
----
1. Approximately how many employees are on your payroll?_____

2. Do you have any kind of dependent care assistance plan available
    to your employees?   Yes_____ No_____

3. If yes, what is the arrangement and are these services for child-
    and/or eldercare?   <u>Childcare</u>   <u>Eldercare</u>
    a. Flexible benefits and
        spending account (cafeteria
        plan)   _____   _____
    b. Referral facilities   _____   _____
    c. On-site care center   _____   _____
    d. Off-site care center   _____   _____
    e. Consortium plan (several   _____   _____
        firms maintain a center)

    f. Public/private partnership   _____   _____
        (your firm commits funds to
        be used for local care and
        referral agencies)

    g. Other (please explain)_____

4. If yes, are your arrangements being used?

    Very little____ Used Moderately_____ Used Extensively_____

5. What product/service does your firm deal in?_____

Bibliography

Allen, Robert E. "It Pays to Invest in Tomorrow's Work Force." *The Wall Street Journal*, November 6, 1989: A16.

Anderson-Ellis, Eugenia. "Elder Care Needn't Keep Employees Out of the Office." *The Wall Street Journal*, August 8, 1988: A14.

"AT&T, Unions Reach Contract Agreement." *Gazette Telegraph*, May, 29, 1989: D1.

Azernoff, Roy S., and Andrew E. Scharlach. "Can Employees Carry the Eldercare Burden?" *Personnel Journal* 67 (September 1988): 60–67.

Bane, MaryJo, Laura Lein, Lydia O'Donnell, C. Ann Sturve, and Barbara Wells. "Child Care Arrangements of Working Parents." *Monthly Labor Review* 102, no. 10 (October 1979): 50–55.

Bardwick, Judith M. *The Plateauing Trap: How to Avoid It in Your Career and Your Life*. New York: AMACOM, 1986.

Barney, Jane L. "The Prerogative of Choice in Long-Term Care." *The Gerontologist* 17, no. 4 (1977): 309–314.

Barrow, Georgia M., and Patricia A. Smith. *Aging, The Individual, and Society*, 2nd ed. St. Paul, Minnesota: West Publishing Company, 1983.

"Benefits Package Set by AT&T, Unions Shows Power of Families in Workplace." *The Wall Street Journal*, May 31, 1989: A6.

Bernstein, Aaron. "Why More Mothers Are Not Married." *Business Week*, May 22, 1989: 74, 75.

Bernstein, Paul. "The Ultimate in Flextime: From Sweden, By Way of Volvo." *Personnel* (June 1988): 70–74.

Bohen, Halcyone H. *Balancing Jobs and Family Life*. Philadelphia: Temple University Press, 1981.

Branch, Laurence G. et al. "Impoverishing the Elderly: A Case Study of the Financial Risk of Spend-Down Among Massachusetts Elderly People." *The Gerontologist* 28, no. 5 (October 1988): 648–652.

Brazelton, T. Berry. *Working and Caring*. Reading, Mass.: Addison-Wesley, 1985.

Brickner, Phillip W. et al. "Home Maintenance for the Home-Bound Aged: A Pilot Program in New York City." *The Gerontologist* 16, no. 1 (1976): 25–29.

Brody, E. M. et al. "Work Status and Parent Care: A Comparison of Four Groups of Women." *The Gerontologist* 27, no. 2 (1987): 201–207.

Bronfenbrenner, Urie. "Strengthening Family Systems," in Edward F. Zigler and Meryl Frank, *The Parental Leave Crisis: Toward a National Policy*. New Haven, Conn.: Yale University Press, 1988: 143–160.

Bureau of National Affairs. *Work and Family: A Changing Dynamic*. Washington, D.C.: 1986.

Burud, Sandra L., Raymond C. Collins, and Patricia Divine-Hawkins. "Employer Supported Child Care: Everybody Benefits." *Children Today* (May-June 1983): 2–7.

"Business Payoffs of Flexible Work Arrangements." *Perspective* (pamphlet). New York: Catalyst Group, September 1989.

Butler, Barbara, and Janis Wasserman. "Parental Leave Attitudes and Practices in Small Businesses," in Edward F. Zigler and Meryl Frank, *The Parental Leave Crisis: Toward A National Policy*. New Haven, Conn.: Yale University Press, 1988: 223–232.

Callahan, James Jr., and Stanley S. Wallack, eds. *Reforming the Long-Term System*. Lexington, Mass.: D. C. Heath and Co., 1981.

Carlson, Elliot. "Long-term Care Woes Dog Many." AARP *Bulletin* 31, no. 2 (February 1990): 1, 5.

Carlson, Eugene. "Small Firms Increasingly Target Market for Parent Care." *The Wall Street Journal*, November 7, 1989: B2.

Catalyst. *The Corporate Guide to Parental Leaves*. New York: Catalyst Group, 1986a.

———. *Report on a National Study of Parental Leaves*. New York: Catalyst Group, 1986b.

Clutterbuck, David, ed. *New Patterns of Work*. Hants, England: Gower Publishing Co. Ltd., 1985.

Cohn, Robert. "A Glimpse of the 'Flex' Future." *Newsweek*, August 1988: 38, 39.

Collins, Sheila K. "Women at the Top of Women's Fields: Social Work, Nursing, and Education," in Anne Statham, et al., eds., *The Worth of Women's Work: A Qualitative Synthesis*. Albany: State University of New York, 1988: 187–201.

"Colorado Day-Care Workers Leave Jobs Over Poor Salaries, Survey Shows." *Gazette Telegraph*, October 11, 1989: B16.

Congressional Record. 134, no. 62. Washington, D.C.: May 5, 1988.

Coontz, Stephanie. "Pro-Family But Divorced from the Facts." *The Wall Street Journal*, August 9, 1989: A10.

Cotten, Terri. "Employees Face Need to Care for Elderly." *Gazette Telegraph*, September, 23, 1989: B1.

Crawford, Bill. "Opportunities Knock." AARP *Bulletin* 31, no. 2 (February 1990): 1, 12.

Creedon, Michael A., ed. *Issues for an Aging America: Employers and Eldercare*. Southport, Conn.: Creative Services, Inc., 1987.

Creedon, Michael A., and Donna L. Wagner. *Eldercare: A Resource Guide*. Bridgeport, Conn.: Center for the Study of Aging, 1986.

Curry, Shirley A. "A Corporate Response: The TRW Experience," in Dallas L. Salisbury, *America in Transition: Implication for Employee Benefits.* Washington, D.C.: Employee Benefit Research Institute, 1982: 55–78.

Daniels, Norman. *Am I My Parent's Keeper?.* New York: Oxford University Press, 1988.

Daniels, R. Steven, Lorin A. Baumhover, and Carolyn L. Clark-Daniels. "Physicians' Mandatory Reporting of Elder Abuse." *The Gerontologist* 29, no. 3 (1989): 321–327.

Davidson, Nicholas. "Dad's Absence Means More than Poverty." *Gazette Telegraph,* January 20, 1990: B9.

"Developing a Flexible Work Arrangements Policy." *Perspective* (pamphlet). New York: Catalyst Group, September 1989.

Diamond, John. "Victory on Child Care Edges Within Reach of Connecticut's Dodd." *Gazette Telegraph,* November 13, 1989: A3.

Dobson, Judith, and Russell L. Dobson. "The Sandwich Generation: Dealing With Aging Parents." *Journal of Counseling and Development* 63 (May 1985): 572–574.

Dunlop, Burton D. "Expanded Home-Based Care for the Impaired Elderly: Solution or Pipe Dream." *American Journal of Public Health* 70, no. 5 (May 1980): 514–519.

Dychtwald, Kenneth, and Joe Flower. *Age Wave: The Challenges and Opportunities of an Aging America.* Los Angeles: Jeremy P. Tarcher, 1989.

Eakes, M. Garey, and Ron M. Landsman. "Medicaid, Money—and You." *Money Magazine* (February-March 1990): 85–90.

Edwards, Richard. *Contested Terrain: The Transformation of the Workplace in the Twentieth Century.* New York: Basic Books, 1979.

Ehrlich, Elizabeth. "The Mommy Track." *Business Week,* March 20, 1989: 126–234.

"Elder Care Affects Jobs, Workers." *Gazette Telegraph,* April 26, 1989.

Ellig, Bruce R. "What's Ahead in Compensation and Benefits." *Management Review* 72 (1983): 56–61.

Employee Benefits in Medium and Large Firms. Washington, D.C.: U.S. Department of Labor, 1986.

Eskow, Dennis. "Firms Turn to Telecommuting." *PC Week* 6 (September 25, 1989): 81, 82.

Fierman, Jaclyn. "Child Care: What Works—and Doesn't." *Fortune,* November 21, 1988: 163–176.

Finegan, Jay. "Deja Vu All Over Again." *INC,* February 1989: 31, 32.

"Firms Offer Emergency Day Care." *Gazette Telegraph,* September 11, 1989: C10.

Fogel, Robert, Elaine Hatfield, Sara B. Kiesler, and Ethel Shanas, eds. *Aging.* New York: Academic Press, 1981.

Foster, Joanna. "Balancing Work and The Family: Divided Loyalties or Constructive Partnership?" *Personnel Management* (September 1988): 39–41.

Frank, Meryl. "Cost, Financing, and Implementation Mechanisms of Parental Leave Policies," in Edward F. Zigler and Meryl Frank, *The Parental Leave Crisis: Toward a National Policy.* New Haven, Conn.: Yale University Press, 1988.

Friedman, Dana E. "Eldercare: The Employee Benefit of the 1990s?" *Across The Board* (June 1986): 45–51.

Garland, Susan B. "Is Medicare a Terminal Case?" *Business Week,* February 5, 1990: 28.

Gibeau, Janice L., Jeane W. Anastas, and Pamela W. Larson. "Breadwinners, Caregivers, and Employers: New Alliance in an Aging America." *Employee Benefits Journal* 12, no. 3 (September 1987): 6–10.

Givner, Bruce. "Cafeteria Plans Need ERISA Protection." *CPA Journal* 57 (December 1987): 89–91.

Glick, Paul, and Sung-Ling Lin. "More Young Adults Are Living With Their Parents: Who Are They?" *Journal of Marriage and the Family* 48 (February 1986): 107–112.

Godwin, Phillip. "Who Will Care for Mom and Dad?" *Better Homes and Gardens*, October 1989: 32, 34.

Gold, Philip. "Bringing Child Care to Work Breaks Home-Office Barriers," *Insight*, March 13, 1989: 40, 41.

Goldscheider, Francis Kobrin, and Celine LeBourdaus. "The Decline in Age at Leaving Home, 1920–1979." *Sociology and Social Research* 70, no. 2 (January 1986): 143–145.

Hagestad, Gunhild O. "The Aging Society as a Context for Family Life." *Daedalus* 115, no. 1 (Winter 1986): 119–139.

Halcrow, Allan. "IBM Answers the Elder Care Need." *Personnel Journal* 67 (September 1988): 67–69.

Hayghe, Howard. "Rise in Mother's Labor Force Activity Includes Those With Infants." *Monthly Labor Review* 109 (February 1986): 44, 45.

Hedges, Janice Neipert, and Daniel E. Taylor. "Recent Trends in Worktime: Hours Edge Downward." *Monthly Labor Review* 103, no. 3 (March 1980): 3–11.

Heer, David M., Robert W. Hodge, and Marcus Felson. "The Cluttered Nest: Evidence That Young Adults Are More Likely to Live at Home Now Than in the Recent Past." *Sociology and Social Research* 69, no. 3 (1985): 436–441.

Hunt, Janet G., and Larry L. Hunt. "The Dualities of Careers and Families: New Integrations or New Polarization?" *Social Problems* 27, no. 5 (1982): 499–510.

Ingersoll-Dayton, Berit, Nancy Chapman, and Margaret Neal. "A Program for Caregivers in the Workplace." *The Gerontologist* 30, no. 1 (1990): 126–130.

Kamerman, Sheila B. *Parenting in An Unresponsive Society: Managing Work and Family Life*. New York: Free Press, 1980.

———. *Parents: A Study of Comparative Policy*. New York: Columbia University Press, 1981.

Kamerman, Sheila B., and Alfred J. Kahn. *The Responsive Workplace: Employers and a Changing Labor Force*. New York: Columbia University Press, 1987.

Kamerman, Sheila B., and Paul W. Kingston. "Employers Responses to the Family: Responsibilities of Employees," in S. B. Kamerman and Cheryl D. Hayes, eds. *Families That Work: Children in a Changing World*. Washington, D.C.: National Academy Press, 1982: 144–208.

Kantrowitz, Barbara, Pat Wingert, and Kate Robbins. "Advocating a 'Mommy Track.'" *Newsweek*, March 13, 1989.

Kocka, Jurgen. *White Collar Workers in America 1890–1940*. Beverly Hills: Sage Publications, 1980.

Kramon, Glenn. "Increasing Health-Care Costs Plague Employers in the U.S." *Gazette Telegraph*, September 24, 1989: D1.

Kutner, Lawrence. "When Young Adults Head Back Home." *New York Times*, July 14, 1988.

"Labor Letter." *The Wall Street Journal*, May 23, 1989: A1.

Lamb, Michael E., ed. *The Father's Role*. New York: John Wiley and Sons, 1986.

Landers, Ann. "Mother's Stroke Robs Daughter of Energy." *Gazette Telegraph*, May 19, 1989: E6.

Larwood, Laurie, Ann H. Stromberg, and Barbara A. Gutek. *Women and Work*. Beverly Hills: Sage Publications, 1985.

Lee, Elliott A. "Firms Begin Support for Workers Who Look After Elderly Relatives." *The Wall Street Journal*, July 6, 1987: 13.

Leib, Jeffrey. "Firms Try Alternatives to Firing Employees." *The Denver Post*, January 29, 1989: G1.

Levine, Hermine Z. "Consensus Child-Care Policies." *Personnel* 61 (March-April 1984): 4–10.

Levy, Gregg. "Consequences of Longevity." *OMNI*, May 9, 1987: 41.

Lewin, Marion Ein, and Sean Sullivan. *The Care of Tomorrow's Elderly*. Washington, D.C.: American Enterprise Institute for Public Policy Research, 1989.

Lewin, Marion Ein, and Stanley Wallack. "Can the Elderly Afford Long-Term Care?" in Marion Ein Lewin and Sean Sullivan, *The Care of Tomorrow's Elderly*. Washington, D.C.: American Enterprise Institute for Public Policy Research, 1989: 161–176.

Lindemann, Dorothy. "A Middle-Aged Child." *U.S. News and World Report*, December 22, 1986: 71.

Littwin, Susan. *The Postponed Generation*. New York: William Morrow, 1986.

Macarov, David. *Worker Productivity: Myths and Reality*. Beverly Hills: Sage Publications, 1982.

Maddox, George L., ed. *The Future of Aging and the Aged*. Atlanta: Southern Newspaper Publishers Association Foundation, 1971.

Marmor, Theodore R. *The Politics of Medicare*, 2nd ed. Chicago: Aldine, 1973.

Martin, Virginia Hider, and Jo Hartley. *Hours of Work When Workers Can Choose*. Washington, D.C.: Business and Professional Women's Foundation, 1975.

Matthews, Sarah H., and Tena Tarler Rosner. "Shared Filial Responsibiltiy: The Family as Primary Caregiver." *Journal of Marriage and Family* 50 (February 1988): 185–195.

McGee, Lynne F. "Setting Up Work at Home . . ." *Personnel Administrator* 33 (December 1988): 58–62.

Mellor, Earl F. "Shift Work and Flextime: How Prevalent?" *Monthly Labor Review* 109 (November 1986).

Meyer, Jack A. "Reforming Medicare and Medicaid," in Marion Ein Lewin and Sean Sullivan, *The Care of Tomorrow's Elderly*. Washington, D.C.: American Enterprise Institute for Public Policy Resarch, 1989: 103–122.

Miller, Dorothy A. "The 'Sandwich Generation': Adult Children of the Aging." *Social Work* 26 (1981): 419–423.

Miller, Thomas I. "The Effects of Employer-Sponsored Child Care on Employee Absenteeism, Turnover, Productivity, Recruitment or Job Satisfaction: What Is Claimed and What Is Known." *Personnel Psychology* 37 (1984): 277–289.

Moon, Marilyn, and Timothy M. Smeeding. "Can the Elderly Afford Long-Term Care?" in Marion Ein Lewin and Sean Sullivan, *The Care of Tomorrow's Elderly*. Washington, D.C.: American Enterprise Institute for Public Policy Research, 1989: 137–160.

Moskowitz, Milton, and Carol Townsend. "The Best Companies For Working Mothers." *Working Mother*, October 1989: 74–100.

Myers, Jane E. "The Mid-Late Life Generation Gap: Adult Children With Aging Parents." *Journal of Counseling and Development* 66 (March 1988): 331–355.

Naisbitt, John. *Megatrends*. New York: Warner Books, Inc., 1984.

Newman, Evelyn S., and Susan R. Sherman. "A Survey of Caretakers in Adult Foster Homes." *The Gerontologist* 17, no. 5 (1977): 436–439.

Nieva, Veronica F. "Work and Family Linkages," in Larwood, Laurie et al., *Women and Work*. Beverly Hills: Sage Publications, 1985: 162–190.

Nollen, Stanley D. "Does Flextime Improve Productivity?" *Harvard Business Review* 57 (September-October 1979): 4–8.

———. "What Is Happening to Flextime, the Variable Day? and Permanent Part-Time Employment? And the Four-Day Week?" *Across The Board* (April 1980): 221–223.

Nussbaum, Karen. "Work and Family: The Issues of Time and Money." Washington, D.C.: Bureau of National Affairs, 1988: 224–226.

Nyborg-Andersen, Irene, and Pamela Guthrie O'Brien. "The Child-Care Patchwork." *Ladies Home Journal*, November 1989: 199–208.

Odiorne, George S. *The Human Side of Management*. Lexington, Mass.: D. C. Heath and Co., 1987.

Otten, Alan L. "As People Live Longer, Houses Become Home to Several Generations." *The Wall Street Journal*, January 27, 1989: A1, 2.

Parnes, Herbert S. *Peoplepower*. Beverly Hills: Sage Publications, 1984.

Patton, Richard E. "Tax Credits For Productivity." *Financial Executive* (January 1983): 34–37.

Peters, Thomas J., and Robert H. Waterman, Jr. *In Search of Excellence*. New York: Harper and Row, 1982.

Petersen, Donald J., "Flextime in the United States: The Lessons of Experience." *Personnel* (January-February 1980): 21–31.

Petersen, Donald J., and Douglas Massengell. "Childcare Programs Benefit Employers, Too." *Personnel* (May 1988): 58–62.

Pleck, Joseph H. "Employment and Fatherhood: Issues and Innovative Policies," in Michael E. Lamb, *The Father's Role*. New York: John Wiley and Sons, 1986: 385–412.

———. "Fathers and Infant Care Leave," in Edward Zigler and Meryl Frank, *The Parental Leave Crisis: Toward a National Policy*. New Haven, Conn.: Yale University Press, 1988: 177–191.

Preston, Samuel H. "Children and the Elderly: Divergent Paths for America's Dependents." *Demography* 21, no. 4 (November 1984): 435–457.

Radigan, Anne L. *Concept and Compromise: The Evolution of Family Leave Legislation in the U.S. Congress*. Washington, D.C.: Women's Research and Education Institute, 1988.

Robertson, Ian. *An Introduction to Sociology*, 3rd ed. New York: Worth Publishers, 1987.

Rodgers, Fran Sussner, and Charles Rodgers. "Business and the Facts of Familiy Life." *Harvard Business Review* 67, no. 6 (November-December 1989): 121–129.

Rosow, Jerome M. "Work and Family: The Productivity Connection," in *Work and Family: A Changing Dynamic*. Washington, D.C.: Bureau of National Affairs, 1986.

Salisbury, Dallas L., ed. *America In Transition: Implication for Employee Benefits.* Washington, D.C.: Employee Benefits Research Institute, 1982.

Sandroff, Ronni. "Why Pro-Family Policies Are Good for Business and America." *Working Woman* (November 1989): 126–131.

" 'Sandwich Generation' Can Benefit From Financial Study During Holidays." *Gazette Telegraph*, November 28, 1989: C12.

Scanlan, B. K. "Determinants of Job Satisfaction and Productivity." *Personnel Journal* 55, 1976.

Schick, Allen. "Health Policy: Spending More and Protecting Less," in Marion Ein Lewin and Sean Sullivan, *The Care of Tomorrow's Elderly.* Washington, D.C.: American Enterprise Institute for Public Policy Research, 1989: 29–52.

Schnaiberg, Allan, and Sheldon Goldenberg. "From Empty Nest to Crowded Nest: The Dynamics of Incompletely-Launched Young Adults." *Social Problems* 36, no. 3 (June 19889): 251–269.

Schreiber, Ronnee. "All in the Family." *Outlook* 83, no. 4. American Association of University Women, 1989: 6, 7.

Schroeder, Patricia. *Champion of the Great American Family.* New York: Random House, 1989.

Segal, Stephen. "The Working Parent Dilemma." *Personnel Journal* 63 (March 1984): 50–56.

Seixas, Suzanne. "Caught Between Grandma and the Kids." *Money* (May 1988): 160–163.

"Senate Takes on Federal Role in Child Care." *The Wall Street Journal*, June 22, 1989: A3.

Sheinberg, Randy. "Parental Leave Policies of Large Firms," in Edward F. Zigler and Meryl Frank. *The Parental Leave Crisis: Toward A National Policy.* New Haven, Conn. Yale University Press, 1988: 211–222.

Sheppard, Harold L., and Sara E. Rix. *The Graying of Working America.* New York: Free Press, 1977.

Sherrod, Pamela. "AT&T, Union Pact Would Break New Ground." *Gazette Telegraph*, June 11, 1989: E5.

Smith, Ralph E., ed. *The Subtle Revolution: Women at Work.* Washington, D.C.: The Urban Institute, 1979.

Smith, Richard M., and Craig W. Smith. "Child Rearing and Single-Parent Fathers." *Family Relations* 29, no. 3 (September 1980): 411–417.

Sommers, Tish, and Laurie Shields. *Women Take Care: The Consequences of Caregiving in Today's Society.* Gainesville, Fla.: Triad Publishing, 1987.

Spalter-Roth, Roberta M., and Heidi I. Hartmann. *Unnecessary Losses: Costs to Americans of the Lack of Family and Medical Leave.* Washington, D.C.: Institute for Women's Research Policy, 1988.

Spalter-Roth, Roberta M., and John Willoughby. "New Workforce Policies and the Small Business Sector: Is Family Leave Good For Business?" Cleveland: 9to5 National Association of Working Women, September 1988.

Stackel, Leslie. "Eldercare: An Emerging Phenomenon." *Employment Relations Today* 13 (Winter 1986–87): 359–364.

"States Help Care for Kids Through Tax Credits and Incentives." *The Wall Street Journal*, January 4, 1989: 1.

Stoiber, Susanne A. *Parental Leave and Women's Place.* Washington, D.C.: Women's Research and Education Institute, 1989.

Stone, Nan. "Mother's Work." *Harvard Business Review* (September-October 1989): 50, 51, 54–56.

Stonebaker, Peter. "A Three-Tier Plan for Cafeteria Benefits." *Personnel Journal* (December 1984): 49–57.

Stuckey, M. Francine, Paul E. McGhee, and Nancy J. Bell. "Parent-Child Interaction: The Influence of Maternal Employment." *Developmental Psychology* 18, no. 4 (1982): 635–644.

Sullivan, Joyce. "Family Support Systems Paychecks Can't Buy." *Family Relations* 30, no. 4 (October 1981): 607–613.

Thompson, Donald B. "Child Care in Reverse." *Industry Week*, August 10, 1987: 28.

Thompson, Ross A. "Fathers and the Child's Best Interests: Judicial Decision Making in Custody Disputes," in Michael E. Lamb, *The Father's Role*. New York: John Wiley and Sons, 1986: 61–102.

Trost, Cathy. "Boss's Backing Vital to Family Benefits." *The Wall Street Journal*, January 19, 1989a: B1.

———. "Few Use Credits for Child-Care Plans, Study Finds." *The Wall Street Journal*, November 14, 1989b: A8, C2.

Velleman, Susan J. "A Benefit to Meet Changing Needs: Child-Care Assistance." *Compensation and Benefits Review* 19 (May-June 1987): 54–58.

Watson, Tony J. *Sociology, Work and Industry*. 2nd ed. London: Routledge & Kegan Paul, 1987.

Wagel, William H. "On the Horizon: HR in the 1990s." *Personnel* 67, no. 1 (January): 11–16.

Weicher, John C. "Wealth and Poverty Among the Elderly," in Marion Ein Lewin and Sean Sullivan, *The Care of Tomorrow's Elderly*. Washington, D.C.: American Enterprise Institute for Public Policy Research, 1989: 11–28.

Weissert, William G., Jennifer M. Elston, Elise J. Boldar, and Cynthia M. Cready. "Models of Adult Day Care: Findings From a National Survey." *The Gerontologist* 27, no. 5 (October 1989): 640–649.

Wessel, David. "With Labor Scarce, Service Firms Strive to Raise Productivity." *The Wall Street Journal*, June 1, 1989: A1.

Winfield, Fairlee E. "Workplace Solutions for Women Under Eldercare Pressure." *Personnel* (July 1987): 31–39.

Winnett, Richard A., and Michael S. Neale. "Results of Experimental Study on Flextime and Family Life." *Monthly Labor Review* (November 1980): 29–32.

Wojahn, Ellen. "Bringing Up Baby: The Myths and Realities of Day Care. *INC*, November 1988: 64–75.

World Development Report. New York: Oxford University Press, 1987, 1988.

Young, Kathryn T., and Edward F. Zigler. "Infant and Toddler Day Care: Regulation and Policy Implications," in Edward F. Zigler and Meryl Frank, *The Parental Leave Crisis: Toward a National Policy*. New Haven, Conn.: Yale University Press, 1988: 120–140.

Zigler, Edward F., and Meryl Frank. *The Parental Leave Crisis: Toward a National Policy*. New Haven, Conn.: Yale University Press, 1988.

Author Index

Subject Index

ABOUT THE AUTHOR

LOUELLEN CRAWFORD is a member of the Affiliate Faculty for Undergraduate and Graduate Programs at Colorado Technical College. Her articles have been published in such periodicals as *The Social Science Journal*, *The Humanist*, and *International Journal of Sociology and Marriage*.